Lien Gw

A Journal of Cornish Folklore

Number 6

Compiled and edited by

Alex Langstone

Spirit of Albion Books

in association with

Lien Gwerin
Kernow
cornishfolklore.co.uk

This collection published in 2022 by Spirit of Albion Books
www.spiritofalbionbooks.co.uk

in association with

Lien Gwerin Kernow www.cornishfolklore.co.uk

Twitter: @CornishFolklore

facebook.com/groups/cornishfolklore

Instagram: lien.gwerin

ISBN 978-1-7398248-0-8

ISSN 2515-2483

© All articles and photographs are copyright to the respective authors. All illustrations are public domain *except* those by Harry Maddox on page 14, Tony Shiels on page 27 and Paul Atlas-Saunders on page 63, which are copyright to the artists

With grateful thanks to:

Paul Atlas-Saunders, Merv Davey, Alan M. Kent, Steve Patterson, Karen F. Pierce, Tony Shiels and Rupert White.

Cover Art:

Detail from the Beast of Bodmin mural by Harry Maddox. Featured in the car park at the rear of The Hole in the Wall pub, Bodmin, Cornwall.

The views and opinions expressed within Lien Gwerin do not necessarily reflect those of the Publisher and/or Editor.

Contents

Illustrations

The Lark in the Morning

Merv Davey

The "Lark in the Morning" is a folk song that enjoys association with a host of quite diverse melodies and its origins are satisfyingly obscure. The broadside ballads of London and the North are easy to trace thanks to the digital archive of the Bodleian Library and the lyrics of the song make several appearances between 1796 and the 1880s courtesy of publishers like Such, Bebbington and Swindells.[1] Most major towns had their own broadside ballad publisher and songs like the "Lark in the Morning" spread far and wide.

The broadside ballads were the pop songs of their day but quite unrestrained by the record labels and copyright of modern times. As part of their sales pitch ballad vendors sang their verses to well-known or catching melodies and so the ballads quickly found their way across the community, entertaining in the taverns or lightening the tedium of repetitive work.

With slight variations the lyrics in the broadside ballads remain essentially the same as those printed by

---

[1] H Such,1863-1885, London Bodleian ref 1188; J.O. Bebbington, Manchester, 1855 -1858, Bodleian ref 13551; Swindells, Manchester 1796-1853, Bodleian ref 16725.

Disley shown here. We have a Bruegelesque picture of country life, of larks singing in the sky, handsome ploughboys, fair maidens, the inevitable tumble in the new mown hay and having to explain the outcome to mum a few months later. We will probably never know if the lyrics were originally coined by one of the broadside balladeers and copied by their contemporaries or whether they had still older origins. The core elements of the story and appreciation of the importance of the ploughboy in agrarian society would certainly have been familiar in the medieval world.

Even by the standard of these broadsides the story line of "Lark in the Morning" is limited, and the verse is but a smidgen above mouth music and nonsense rhymes that provide a medium for the melody. This simplicity may have been part of its charm and the reason for why it connected with so many different tunes. By the time the great folk song collectors, such as Cecil Sharp, George Gardiner, and Percy Grainger, were marching around the countryside dutifully recording the songs of the people the "Lark in the Morning" was part of a living tradition embedded in communities across Britain, Ireland and beyond.[2]

"The Lark in the Morning" became part of the folk revival repertoire and in turn was picked up by the folk bands in the 60s and 70s. The Dubliners regaled us with a lively melody and the principal characters acquired the names Roger and Susan. Steeleye Span provided a completely different tune and haunting

---

[2] For example, the Cecil Sharp, Percy Grainger and George Gardiner Collections held by the Vaughan Williams Memorial Library Cecil Sharp House. https://www.vwml.org/.

arrangement. Both groups understandably dropped the "As I walked out one May Morning" introductory verse as this had become the ubiquitous entrée for so many folk songs.

THE
Lark in the Morning

H. Disley, Printer; 57, High-street, St. Giles.

As I was a walking one morning in May
I heard a pretty damsel these words for to say,
Of all the callings whatever they may be,
No life is like the ploughboy in the merry month of May

The lark in the morning awakes from her nest,
And mounts the white air with the dew round her breast,
And like the pretty ploughboy she'll whistle and sing,
And at night she'll return to her nest again

When his' day's work is done that he hath to do,
Perhaps to a fair or a wake will he go,
There with his sweetheart, he'll dance and he'll sing
And then he will return with his lass back again.

And as they return from the wake in the town,
The meadows being mown, and the grass cut down,
We chanced to tumble all on the new mown hay-
It's kiss me now or never the maiden did say.

When twenty weeks were over and past,
Her mamma ask'd her the reason why she so
Thickened in the waist?
It was the pretty ploughboy, the damsel did say,
That caused me to tumble on the new-mown hay.

Come all ye pretty maidens, whereever you be,
You may trust a ploughboy to any degree;
They're used so much to ploughing, their seed for to sow
That all employ them are sure to find it grow.

So Good I luck to the ploughboys wherever they be,
They will I take a sweet maiden to sit on thire knee,
And with a jug of beer, they will whistle and sing,
And the ploughboy is as happy as a prince or a king.

The song was known in Cornwall long before the Dubliners and Steeleye Span, and we have our own distinctive melodies to go with it. My favourite must be the deliciously spine-tingling tune used by Anna Dowling and Jane Cox in the soundtrack introducing Alex Langstone's "From Granite to Sea".[3] Quite when the song arrived in Cornwall, we do not know but by the time Rev Sabine Baring Gould set out on his folk song collecting expeditions in the 1890s it was sufficiently well established to have connected with more than one tune.

In July 1891 Baring Gould and his colleague Rev Frederick Bussel knocked at the door of the Falcon Inn[4] and introduced themselves. They were greeted with great delight by Miss Gilbert, the landlord's daughter *"we have been so longing for you to come. Dear old father, now nearly ninety, used to be such a singer, and my sister and I, when we heard you were collecting the old songs, have over and over again wished you would come here and take down father's sweet old ditties before they were lost."* [5]

The two gentlemen stayed for three days noting down songs from the elderly Sam Gilbert and a number of other people from the area.[6] Bussel was a trained musician and would transcribe the music score while Baring Gould took down the words, asking their singers

---

[3] Alex Langstone, From Granite to Sea, Troy Books: www.troybooks.co.uk
[4] The Falcon Inn, St Mawgan in Pydar (Editor's note)
[5] Sabine Baring Gould, Notes On Songs *A Garland of Country Song*, (London, Methuen & Co, 1895). P vii Baring-Gould, Garland of Country Song (1895) pp.58-59
[6] Graebe, October, The Folk Next Door: Sabine Baring-Gould and Cornwall, Paper presented at the Baring Gould Weekend, Okehampton, 20th Oct 2001

to repeat until they were satisfied that it had been taken down correctly. It is easy to imagine these two holding court at the Falcon, and probably plying their singers with drinks, while word circulated the neighbourhood. Sam Gilbert provided them with the lyrics for "The Lark in the Morning" and one of the tunes that went with them. John Old of St Eval provided him with another, quite different tune.

Sam Gilbert sung a reduced version of the lyrics from those known elsewhere and in his notes Baring Gould comments that he is not sure whether this was because Sam had forgotten them or thought they were too coarse. The missing verses concern "tumbling in the hay" and the allusion to the ploughboy's "seed" and one can well imagine Sam not wishing to sing this in front of the two reverends! Baring Gould went on to publish Sam Gilbert's version of the song in his Garland of Country Songs in 1895, [7] where it was introduced to a wider audience and joined by other versions as they were published in due course. John Old's tune, however, remained forgotten between the covers of Baring Gould's notebooks.

Baring Gould's methodology was to use rough copy notebooks to capture tunes and lyrics in the field and then tidy them up with additional notes and references in fair copies from which he selected those which he went on to publish. John Old's tune is written out just once in a rough copy notebook and then again

---

[7] Sabine Baring Gould, *A Garland of Country Song*, (London, Methuen & Co, 1895) pp.58-59

along with the other tunes and the lyrics in a fair copy.[8] Apart from one note which is sharpened the notes remain in the same position on the stave and with the same values between the rough copy and the fair copy. Baring Gould, however, added three flats to the key signature in the fair copy completely changing the mood of the tune.

Baring Gould's biographer, Martin Greabe, points out that in a scientific sense there is not enough data in Baring Gould's manuscripts for certainty. We do not know for sure which is the version that Sabine Baring Gould and Frederick Bussell heard John Old sing. If Bussel made the original transcription in the rough notebook then he was a trained musician, and one would expect this to be the correct one, but it is upside down on the page and indeed quite "rough". Did Baring Gould simply correct the tune in his fair copy to what he remembered, or did he make what he felt were improvements to the tune? It was neither unknown nor thought to be wrong to do this with traditional music in Baring Gould's day.

In 1974 Gordon Hitchcock arranged and published a collection drawn from Baring Gould's notebooks called "Folk Songs of the West Country"[9] and included "The Lark in the Morning" with both Sam

---

[8] Baring Gould Rough Copy Notebook 3, Wren Trust ref SBG 3-6; Baring Gould Faircopy, Wren Trust ref SBG 3-1. Baring Gould's manuscripts were catalogued by the Wren Trust and are held partly by the Devon Archive and Partly Plymouth Library. Some manuscripts are digitised and can be viewed online at the Vaughan Williams Memorial Library Website: www.vwml.org
[9] Gordon Hitchcock. Folk Songs of the West Country, (Newton Abbot: David & Charles: Keith Prowse Music Publishing Co., 1974), pp.70 – 73.

9

Gilbert's tune and the version of John Old's tune in Baring Gould's fair copy manuscript. Hitchcock arranged the tune so that it better fitted the words and also added some embellishments of his own. [10]

A Breton Band called Lyonesse recorded Gordon Hitchcock's version of John Old's tune in 1975. Here it is arranged with bombardes and pipes and joins another Cornish song "The Three Knights". It was translated into Cornish as "An Awhesyth – The Lark" in the late 1970s [11], it also became a popular as an instrumental tune in its own right and was included in the Racca, Cornish session tune project in 1995. Dalla recorded "The Lark in the Morning" in their K5 Album released in 2013.

Although we can follow the songs trajectory after Baring Gould's visit to the Falcon Inn, and how the tunes and lyrics have been arranged and adapted since then, we know little of them before this date except that it was sung by Sam Gilbert and his friends in their younger days. This places the lyrics to the mid-1850s when the broadside ballads were circulating but tells us little about the melodies and the musical culture that went with them. John Old's tune as played by Lyonesse is enticingly at home with the Breton style of arrangement, does it have its origins in the shared cultural history of Brittany and Cornwall? Did John Old create the tune himself? Although Baring Gould saw his singers as purveyors of a musical heritage

---

[10] Lyonesse – Lyonesse Pathe Marconi Emi Label:PDU – 2C 064-96093, Vinyl, LP, Album, Stereo

[11] Merv Davey, Hengan (Redruth Dyllansow Truran, 1983)

rather than creative singers in their own right, this was his class prejudice.

The wider social milieu of working-class Cornwall in the late 19th century was both musically literate and creative. I have an image in my head of John Old hearing of the two Reverend gentleman holding court at the Falcon and thinking to himself "I can find a tune in my head that is worth a pint"!

Visit the Cornish national music archive for more information and listen to the song.

The Cornish National Music Archive aims to collect information about musical cultures in Cornwall and its diasporic communities; from step-dancing to brass bands, electronica to folk sessions, and Christmas carols to bagpipes. It is for everybody to use, to learn from, and to contribute to.

www.cornishnationalmusicarchive.co.uk

Bizarre Beasts of Cornwall

Alex Langstone

Somewhere between the eldritch realm of Forteana and the conceptual ideas of folk horror lies a peculiar domain of extreme strangeness which has richly inspired the research surrounding this article. The bizarre beasts of Cornwall is a world of weird, where if you expect the unusual and can momentarily leave the world of reason behind, will reveal a rich and wondrous seam of folklore, navigating across a period of three hundred years. From the 1720s in Ladock, through the Victorian era and throughout the twentieth century; and finally bringing us up to date with odd tales still being reported in 2021.

Of course, the Cornish folklore archive is full of sightings of sea serpents, mermaids, and dragons, but there are denizens of other odd creatures to be found, if you seek at the edge.

The most famous of all the modern strange beasts must be the *Beast of Bodmin*. As I write this, local newspaper *The Cornish Guardian* has the headline "Big Cat Encounter", which goes on to describe the most recent of confrontation with the alien big cat of Bodmin Moor, where a creature the size of a giant lurcher was seen on the cycle path known as Walter's trail on the Lanhydrock estate, near Bodmin. This trail is densely wooded, and deer are often seen in the area. The big cat was described as dark charcoal grey, with a tail around 60 centimetres long and bushy fur. This means the cat would have stood around 76 centimetres in height.[12] The witness described the incident as odd and surreal but felt that the big cat was out hunting deer, as he had seen several just prior to the cat's appearance.

There have been around sixty sightings of the Bodmin Beast recorded in the area since 1983, and a spate of recent sightings, such as the one reported above, keeps the tale alive. 'The phantom cat' is frequently thought to be a Lynx, Leopard or Panther, and in 1995 a skull was found by the River Fowey, measuring about 10 cm long by 18 cm wide. Although lacking its lower jaw, it possessed two sharp, prominent

---

[12] Cornish Guardian, 25th August 2021

teeth that suggested that it might have been a leopard. The story hit the national press at about the same time of the official denial of alien big cat evidence on Bodmin Moor. The skull was sent to the Natural History Museum in London for verification. They determined that it was a genuine skull from a young male leopard, but also found that the cat had not died in Britain and that the skull had been imported as part of a leopard-skin rug.[13]

The legend of the Beast of Bodmin is still commemorated today within the annual folk-tradition of Bodmin Riding. This ancient patronal feast of the old trade guilds is still held each July. The origins of Bodmin Riding can be traced to 1469, which suggests

---

[13] From Granite to Sea by Alex Langstone, pp 141-142

that the festival is one of the oldest surviving calendar customs in Cornwall and both celebrates and commemorates some of the towns historical and mythological themes. The revival of the Riding has woven the old trade guild traditions with a collection of folklore from Halgavor Moor and the modern myth of the beast of Bodmin. It is here that we find the Beast, who is hunted by guise costumed local youths, known as the Helliers, and brought to trial in a contemporary mystery play known as An Gwary Bosvena.

Bodmin continues to promote the tales of the Beast, and there is a recent town centre mural *(see previous page)* depicting the folkloric creature, painted by local artist Harry Maddox, in all his splendour. The artwork is also emblazoned on the front cover of this publication.

There is a far stranger account of a mysterious beast that was once sighted in the village of St Mawgan, close to Newquay airport. In the lush and beautiful Vale of Lanherne, where the River Menalhyl (Cornish language: melyn [mill] and heyl [estuary]) persists in her eternal flow towards the Celtic Sea. Here lies a bizarre modern mystery. It is one of those persistent elements from the past that crop up in the local press from time to time. One of those weird things that seem to creep up from the tenacity of a shared cultural memory. The case of the Woodwose of St Mawgan was first recorded by Cryptozoology researcher Deborah Hatswell, and subsequently listed on her *British*

Wildman Sightings map. [14] The story was later picked up by *Cornwall Live* on 12th September 2020. The tale is told by an anonymous estate worker who nervously recounts his memories of the event, which took place just over twenty years ago somewhere in the Vale of Lanherne. This would place the incident sometime during the late 1990s, and it is told something like this:

Bigfoot Spotted in St Mawgan Woods!

The eyewitness was working in woodland, making wooden pheasant cages, when he saw something which scared him. It happened towards the end of the working day, whilst waiting for his boss to arrive to take him home. As he waited, he began to hear loud knocks and whistles coming from the surrounding woods. Whilst pondering on what kind of bird could make the noises, he scanned the forest edges, seeking possible origins of the sudden disturbance. Then suddenly he became aware that something was watching him, and he saw an inexplicable face loom from the undergrowth. He moved forward to gain a better view and was astonished when a very strange looking creature emerged from the vegetation. He described it as a male humanoid, around 2 metres tall, and almost completely covered with copper coloured fur.

14

www.google.com/maps/d/viewer?mid=1s1zOmmdM216PMftPUM9K1qqGrFg&ll=
50.40069340081982%2C-4.689857093591103&z=9

From the description he gives of the area, it is probable that it was somewhere on the Carnanton Estate, most likely at Carnanton Woods. The eerie tale continues, where the witness describes how his boss duly picked him up, and how he eventually gained enough courage to ask him about the extraordinary sighting. His boss then casually replied *"Oh yes, we call them Woodwose here, best to just leave them be".*[15]

Curiously, at the south-eastern end of the Vale of Lanherne in the parish church at St Columb Major there are bench ends featuring strange creatures and

---

[15] Cornwall Live: www.cornwalllive.com/news/cornwall-news/day-bigfoot-stalked-workers-cornwall-4504485

grotesque heads, and close by at St Eval, the church has several green man designs placed on some of the roof bosses. Maybe these old carvings were deliberately positioned nearby to remind us of a lost localised ancient folk narrative of something wild and mysterious; the remnants of which, may still survive today in the nearby woods.

Taken at face value, this report seems ludicrous. But is it that dissimilar to comparable, more historic tales from the canon of Cornish folklore? It is not the only folk narrative that describes mysterious creatures in St Magwan. In 1827 the Royal Cornwall Gazette ran a report about a group of gruesome looking mermaids

Mawgan Porth Beach, a gathering place of mermaids?

that had been observed on the rocks and in the caves at Mawgan Porth. These reports came from various witnesses across several days. Here is the full report:

Mermaids on the Coast of Cornwall - The following is an extract of a letter received on Sunday 1ˢᵗ July from our Correspondent at St. Columb': "Within these last two or three days there have been several mermaids seen on the rocks at Trenance, in the parish of Mawgan. I will state the particulars at length, as I have been enabled to collect them, and which are from undoubted authority, and you can make what extracts you think proper. One evening this week, a young man from the adjoining the beach at Mawgan Porth, had made an appointment to meet another person on the beach to catch sprats with him. He went out about ten o'clock at night and coming near a point which runs into the sea, he heard a screeching noise proceeding from a large cavern which is left by the tide at low water, but which has some deep pools in it, and communicates with the sea by another outlet. He thought it was the person he had appointed to meet, and called out to him, but his astonishment is not to be described when on going up he saw something in the shape of a human figure staring on him, with long hair hanging all around its body. He then ran away, thinking, as he went, that he had seen the devil. The next day, some men being on the cliffs near this place, saw three creatures of the same description. The following day five were seen. The persons who saw the last five describe them in this manner: The mermaids were about forty feet below the men (who stood on the cliff), and were lying on a rock, separated from the land some yards by deep water; two of them were large, about four feet and a half to five feet long, and these appeared to be sleeping on the rock; the other small ones were swimming about, and went off once to sea and then came back again. The men looked at them for more than an hour, and flung stones at them, but they would not move off. The large ones seemed to be lying on their faces, their upper parts were like those of human beings, and black or dark-coloured, with very long hair hanging around them; their lower parts were of a bluish colour, and terminating in a fin, like fish. The sea would sometimes wash over them, and then leave them dry again. Their movements seemed to be slow. The hair of these mermaids extended to a distance of nine or ten feet."[16]

These mermaids do not sound like the usual description of beautiful young maids with fish tails, but rather something more sinister. Interestingly, there were nine distinct sightings of these creatures over three days. However, the description of the 'mermaids' on the rocks would fit the descriptions of seals, and the appearance of wild long hair was more than likely seaweed. However, a fascinating report, and it is easy to imagine the tall tales that were subsequently circulated after a glass or two of strong ale, huddled around the blazing hearth in St Mawgan's village pub, the Falcon Inn.

---

[16] Report from the Royal Cornwall Gazette, Saturday 7th July 1827.

Moving a short distance further along the north coast, there is a curious tale that was once told about the ghost of a dog headed man at Harlyn. This was recorded by surrealist artist and occultist Ithell Colquhoun, whilst on a trip to visit the owners of the historic Harlyn House *(right)* during the 1950s. Colquhoun was seeking the strange and unusual, and questioned Captain Millar and his

family, who had been living in the house since 1946, about any resident ghosts. Amid the cosier tales of a spectral white cat who was reputed to haunt the gardens and that of a former maid who was occasionally seen on the stairs, came the gruesome description of the Dog Headed Man who is sometimes seen at daybreak, where he appears to guard the front avenue and main entrance of the house during the twilight hours before dawn. A tradesman once reported that he could not bear to work at Harlyn House anymore because each morning, upon his early arrival, he would be greeted by a hideous apparition which had the appearance of a dog/man hybrid.[17] Interestingly, Harlyn House is also reported as being haunted by a spectral black dog, and this was recounted as residing in the house, probably

---

[17] The Living Stones by Ithell Colquhoun, p 133

as the guardian ghost of the Peter family, who had continuously lived in the house between the 1630s and 1856.[18]

Incidentally, the tale of the dog headed man reminds me of one of the first and scariest folkloric narratives that I encountered as an 11-year-old child. Whilst watching the legendary, and now much talked about BBC Nationwide broadcast of 20th February 1976, archaeologist Dr Anne Ross was interviewed about the case of the Northumbrian Hexham Heads.[19] It was on this programme that she revealed that she had been haunted by sinister visitations of werewolves at her home. She recalled one particular incident of being awoken from a deep sleep to see several werewolves leaving her bedroom and padding downstairs, leaping over the banister and congregating around the front door before exiting. Ross described one of the creatures:

"It was about six feet high, slightly stooping, and was black against the white door. It was half-animal and half-man. The upper part, I would have said, was a wolf, and the lower part was human... It was covered with a very dark fur."[20]

---

[18] "The Black Dog" By Theo Brown. Folklore, vol. 69, no. 3, 1958, p 184
[19] Quest for the Hexham Heads by Paul Screeton
[20] Scarred for Life Volume 1: The 1970s by Stephen Brotherstone and Dave Lawrence, pp 735 - 737

Interestingly, like the Dog Man of Harlyn, these creatures appeared to congregate around entrances and exits of the buildings they seemed to inhabit.

Indeed, 1976 seems to have been a year of bizarre monster manifestations and we can't leave the topic without mentioning two of the most notorious modern-day Cornish crypto-monsters; Morgawr and Owlman, and the man at the very epicentre of their mythology; surrealist magician Tony 'Doc' Shiels.

During the hot summer of '76 'Doc' Shiels and friends appeared to upturn reality and conjure two of Falmouth's most arcane spirits, the sea serpent Morgawr and the Owlman of Mawnan.

In the years since there have been sporadic sightings of both creatures, and I have reports and press cuttings from the Summer of 1995, where a spate of rumours suggested that both serpent and Owlman were once again materialising along the Falmouth coastline. Morgawr was witnessed at various locations, including the Helford Passage, Mawnan Church and Portscatho.[21]

Around the same time the *Black Panther of Rame* was spotted at Antron Hill, between Long Downs and Mabe Burnthouse. The large black cat was seen in the headlights standing in the road and running along the hedge line, keeping up with the car, before leaping

---

[21] Falmouth Packet, 28th September 1995

over a fence on the opposite side of the road, where it disappeared into the undergrowth.

The most recent sighting of Morgawr that I have in my archives is from Summer 2005, where a local man was out in a boat on the River Fal at Philleigh. He was just passing Smuggler's Cottage when he saw what he thought was a seal's head poking out of the water. He pointed it out to his companion, and they turned the boat towards it. Once they had got close, the head submerged, along with two serpentine humps, which he described as looking like black car tyres. He immediately thought of the Loch Ness Monster, and much later, after discussing the strange experience, he realised that he had witnessed Morgawr. [22]

However, despite the many modern sightings of a sea serpent in Cornish waters, Morgawr does have some history to her many appearances all around Cornwall's stunningly rugged and atmospheric shore. One of the earliest reports comes from the latter part of the nineteenth century in North Cornwall. On the 11th October 1882 a sea-serpent was seen off the coast at Bude by local vicar, Rev. E Highton, along with several friends. It was mid-afternoon and they were walking along the gloriously sandy Summerleaze beach. They were stopped in their tracks when they observed a long low dark object skimming across the calm surface of the ocean. They estimated that it was travelling at around 25 *mph* and never once disappeared from view. On one

---

[22] Author's archive

occasion a greater mass appeared above the water, and they all saw a tail, which looked like it was curling in towards the long thin body of the creature. Its length was reported to be between 50 – 80 feet.[23]

Meanwhile, whilst many were witnessing a mid-1990s resurgent Morgawr around the bay, Owlman seemed to make a brief return at Mawnan Woods. Apparently described by a marine-biology student from Chicago, who witnessed the surreal monster whilst holidaying in the area. The Owlman evidently spotted her whilst she was out walking, and she explained how the monster arose and floated towards her. [24]

She described him as: *"a vision from hell, with a ghastly face, a wide mouth, glowing eyes and pointed ears. It also had clawed wings and was covered with silvery-grey feathers. The creature also had large bird legs with huge black claws"*

There are other, similar tales of strange and sinister birds in the Cornish folklore archive. Sometime during late May 1926, it was reported that two boys from Porthtowan witnessed a huge bird which was described as 6 foot 3 inches from tip of the one wing to the other and was three feet in length. It had a powerful pointed beak, six inches in length with large, webbed feet, striped with green and yellow, and a duck shaped

---

[23] The Times, 12th October 1882
[24] Falmouth Packet, 7th September 1995

body. The plumage was of cream colour, tinged with brown on the beak, and also on the upper wing coverts, and the tips of the wings were black. The report from the Cornish Echo, went on to recount the strange tale, stating that the two lads saw this striking bird flapping about on the top of a mine burrow. The youngest boy went to investigate and discovered that the bird was severely injured, and he thought it was dead. However, the bird sprang to life and attacked him. The older boy joined him and managing to defend himself with a stick, covered the bird with his coat, trying to subdue it, but the strange avian creature still managed to bite his hand. Many of the villagers came to view the bird, but none recognised the species. The feathered beast appeared to be in a very poor state of health, and due to rapid decay was soon buried. [25]

Another interesting piece of Porthtowan folklore can be found at the other side of the village at Mile Hill. This tale concerns a fearsome fire-breathing dragon, who once made its lair up on the hilltop, between Chapel Hill and Nancekuke Common. The dragon regularly stalked the area seeking food of sheep and cattle, terrifying the community, and fiercely marking its territory. However, on one particular night on the eve of May and close to midnight, a ghostly black and white spotted dog who haunted the nearby lanes and coombes appeared. He was on the hunt for the dragon and soon found it eating one of the local farmer's sheep.

---

[25] Cornish Echo, 4th June 1926. Page 6

He squared up to the dragon and let out a long low growl. The dragon started to move in readiness to strike the dog, but the ghost dog sank its teeth into the

Dog and Dragon by Tony Shiels.

dragons' tail, ripping the tip clean off. The monster let out a fiery roar and the dog chased it towards the cliffs and the dragon flew off into the sea, never to be seen again. The black and white ghost dog is still sometimes witnessed in the area. Appearing after dark, he stalks the narrow lanes around Porthtowan, and in particular on the old liminal festive nights of Halloween, Candlemas, May Eve, Midsummer, Midwinter and Lammas, seemingly making him a spectral guardian of the turning tides across the year [26]

There is a curious and historic point of interest worthy of addition to this wonderful folktale. During the early 1970s, Tony 'Doc' Sheils' family owned the Woodland restaurant at Mile Hill and 'Doc' persuaded his parents to rename the venue *The Dog & Dragon'*. It wasn't long before adverts and signage were sporting his wonderfully imaginative and graphic artwork of the folk narrative, enabling locals and visitors alike to marvel at the intricacies of Porthtowan's very own otherworldly and spooky folktale.[27]

Another demon-bird-hybrid appeared in the village of Ladock sometime during the early eighteenth century. The folklore was recorded by William Bottrell and is reproduced below:

A very large bird was spotted atop the tower of Ladock parish church. It was described as having coal black plumage, with fiery-red glowing eyes. None of the Ladock residents could recognise the bird and was seen perched on the tower for several nights in succession,

---

[26] Ghosts of Cornwall by Peter Underwood, pp 68, 69
[27] Monstermind: The Magical Life and Art of Tony 'Doc' Shiels by Rupert White

where it remained for hours jumping from one pinnacle to another, and making an unnatural clamour, which was heard for many miles around. The local vicar of the time was the famous ghost-laying, exorcist and astrologer Parson Wood. William Wood was rector at Ladock between 1704 and 1749, a time when many Cornish clergy were involved in lavish exorcisms of demons and ghosts. Rev. Wood was a skilled exorcist, astrologer and occultist and he was kept busy keeping many undesirable entities at bay. He quickly set about dispelling this avian-demon, who he was sure had been sent by the witches of nearby St Enoder. Eventually Rev. Wood expelled the beast, sending him back to the St Enoder witches, who could often be seen flying on their ragwort stems during the time of the full moon or heading home after their midnight meetings in the shape of hares. 28

28 Stories and folk-lore of West Cornwall by William Bottrell (1880), pp 9, 12 - 13

There are a few other Cornish strange beastie sightings that are worth mentioning before we close. Menacuddle Well (below) lies on the edge of St Austell in a lush green valley. The baptistery dates to the 14th

century and the well's waters have magical qualities as was reported in Hope's Legendary Lore of the Holy Wells of England:

The virtues of these waters are very extraordinary, but the advantages to be derived from them are rather attributed to the sanctity of the fountain than to the natural excellence of its stream. Weak children have frequently been carried here to be bathed; ulcers have also been washed in its sacred water, and people in season of sickness have been recommended by the neighbouring matrons to drink of

 this salubrious fluid. In most of these cases, instances may be procured of benefits received from the application, but the prevailing opinion is that the advantages enjoyed result rather from some mystical virtue attributed to the waters for ages past, than from the natural qualities. Within the memory of persons now living, this well was a place of general resort for the young and thoughtless. On approaching the margin, each visitor, if he hoped for good luck through life, was expected to throw a crooked pin into the water, and it was presumed that the other pins which had been deposited there by former devotees might be seen rising from their beds, to meet it before it reached the bottom, and though many have gazed with eager expectation, no one has yet been permitted to witness this extraordinary phenomenon.

Modern folklore records an eerie out-of-place creature living near the well, and a few years ago when the well and gardens were being restored, it was spotted. Subsequently described as a large dark and mysterious monster, weirdly shaped, with an eerie and sinister face. The creature is believed to be living nearby in the dense thickets of this deep granite valley. A local resident described the creature as a large black animal which neither looked like a dog or a cat and went on to warn the volunteers to be careful clearing the trees as it had often been glimpsed prowling around at dusk.[29]

There are many other locations where strange and uncanny creatures have been seen over the years. There have been reports of a strange jumping creature, reputed to haunt the coast near Falmouth, between Swanpool and Maenporth. Described as slightly larger than a dog, with cat's face, walking on its hind legs.[30] The beast of Perrancoombe, which has been described equally as a red eyed creature seen in the woods at night, and as an odd-looking dog-like creature with a human face seen walking along the road after dark. [31] Also, the *Red Cat* of Mevagissey, which was blamed for a spate of carcasses of several deer that appeared to have been partially eaten.

So, what are these creatures, and what to make of it all. Are they paranormal manifestations, escaped

[29] St Austell Voice 29th July 2015

[30] www.paranormaldatabase.com/cornwall/pages/corndata.php?pageNum_paradata=2&totalRows_paradata=317

[31] 1995. Personal correspondence with local resident

pets, or something else? The world of Cryptozoology may give some answers. Examples include mis-identification (Beast of Bodmin) and zooform phenomenon (Harlyn Dog Man).

Nevertheless, I believe that it is of significant value to bring these eighteenth, nineteenth, twentieth and twenty-first century folkloric narratives together so we can compare and contrast the 'paranormal contemporary legends' with the older - and no less outlandish - established folklore. It is good to remember that legends are as powerful as any truth, and whilst some may find sightings of a Cornish Bigfoot completely untenable, the tale is now out there in the folkloric , sitting collectively with the other equally bizarre stories from across the centuries.

Further reading:

The Owlman and Others by Jonathan Downes

Monstrum: A Wizard's Tale by Tony 'Doc' Shiels

Monstermind: The Magical Life and Art of Tony 'Doc' Shiels by Rupert White

The Living Stones by Ithell Colquhoun

TFG Dexter: Cornish Pagan

Rupert White

The period between the wars saw a re-evaluation of common-sense views regarding the religious history of Britain. In Cornwall, no-one was more outspoken in this regard than Thomas F G Dexter who, in vigorously promoting the pagan legacy of the Duchy, was considered something of a heretic by many of his peers.

Dexter's biographical details are scanty. Born in 1860 in South London, he had a wife called Eulalie, and between 1898 and 1905 was the author of four textbooks for trainee teachers, as well as a pioneering work on educational psychology (Dexter and Garlick, 1902). In an advert for one of these titles he is described as the Headmaster of Finsbury Pupil Teacher's School in Barnsbury, Islington (Cornishman Obituary, October 1933)[32].

Having first visited Cornwall at the age of 30 (Dexter & Dexter, 1938) Dexter started taking an interest in its antiquities and became convinced that the remains of the old church of Perranzabuloe could be found, and uncovered, somewhere in the vast sand dunes to the east of Perranporth beach.

---

[32] In 1908 the Educational Times indicates that, that year, he moved to become Principal of Islington Day College in Offord Road.

TFG Dexter stood outside the main entrance to St Piran's Oratory, the earliest of three churches built in Perranzabuloe. The second church, found and excavated by Dexter, had been sited three hundred yards from it and further inland, in the hope that the sands blowing up from the beach could not inundate it quite so easily.

The old church was last used in 1790 before being dismantled and moved to its new, current site further inland. It had been built in the 11th century to replace the even older oratory of St Piran which is the primitive stone structure nearby. Both the old church and the oratory had fallen victim to the beach's shifting sands, but the much-celebrated oratory, with its enigmatic stone carvings, had been excavated again in 1840.

In the summer of 1917, at the age of 57, Dexter started work in the dunes, and, sure enough successfully dug out - by hand - the remains of the old church with the help of a small band of trusty volunteers[33]. Based on his efforts, he was awarded a PhD by St Andrews, and his carefully written report on the excavation can be seen at the Royal Cornwall Museum (RIC).

A few years later, also under the auspices of the Royal Institution of Cornwall (RIC), Longmans published Dexter's 'Cornish names', (Dexter, 1926) a detailed but accessible explanation of hundreds of Cornish place-names that draws on an extensive knowledge of the Cornish language.

It was in the last few years of his life that Dexter's books on paganism were published, however, and in what appears a complete volte-face given his previous work[34], in all of them he seems determined to demonstrate that Christianity in Britain was but a thin and rather feeble veneer over a much more substantial

---

[33] This, together with the fact that Dexter can be shown to have become more involved in the RIC and RCPS in 1919, suggests he retired early to Cornwall either during or immediately after WW1.
[34] His work on place-names probably helped uncover this hidden history though WW1 may have caused him to have a crisis of faith.

pagan history. It was an idea that was considered subversive at the time.

To

William T. Mitchell Esqre.

In memory of the Summers of 1917, 1918 & 1919, and of much valued co-operation in the excavation of the Old Parish Church of Perranzabuloe.

J. F. G. Dexter,

New Year's Day, 1921.

Dedication on the inside cover of Dexter's report on the old church of Perranzabuloe, now held by the RIC. William Mitchell appears to have been one of his assistants. Dexter conducted guided tours in the dunes for several years afterwards.

In 1929 a quartet of self-published works appeared. 'Civilisation in Britain', 'The Sacred Stone', 'The Pagan Origin of Fairs' and 'Fire Worship in Britain' all ask probing questions about Britain's pagan past. The latter, for example, describes the Celtic and solar fire festivals and notes their survival into modern times. Not only does Dexter explain that some of the most important dates in the Christian calendar are

37

derived from these festivals, but that several saints, most obviously St Bridget, are in fact pagan gods. He even suggests, for example, that the names St Anne and St Antony actually refer to Tan the pagan fire-god. Referring to St Anthony in Roseland says: *it may be that we have here another Lan-tinn-ey, 'Enclosure of the Fire' and this surmise receives support from the fact that there is today a lighthouse on the point, for it would seem that man of old like man today saw the necessity of a beacon light on this promontory....The Cornish Anthonys just noted would seem to be but clerical equations for the fire-god Tin, Ten, Tan in his sacred enclosure.*

'The Sacred Stone', adopts a similar approach, and refers to Dexter's preferred theory that settlers from the Mediterranean built some of our most famous monuments (=diffusion theory): *Our stone circles are believed to have been erected by sun-worshippers, our cromlechs by those who practised the cult of the dead, and both circle and cromlech seem to have been built by metal-seekers...Sun-worship, cult of dead and metal seeking all point to the East, and preferably to Egypt but the claims of Mesopotamia and of the Eastern Mediterranean must not be forgotten.* Supporting this Dexter notes a possible physical resemblance between some Celtic crosses and the Egyptian ankh.

A fifth 'pagan' publication, 'Cornwall: Land of the Gods' (1932), takes up the same themes but addresses Cornish prehistory more specifically, challenging accounts by the likes of Baring-Gould and other hagiographers regarding the nature of the Celtic Saints: *Cornwall has about 4000 years of history. It is* generally supposed that Christianity was introduced into Cornwall sometime in the fifth century. So, of the 4000 years of Cornish history 2,500 are pagan and only 1,500 Christian. The history of Christianity in Cornwall has been well explored, but few if any have essayed to deal with the 2,500 years of paganism...the plea of this book is that it is our business to find out something about it......

Long before the birth of Christ the mid-winter festival of the sun-god Mithras was kept on Dec. 25th...the popular holiday on Dec 25th was continued not as a celebration of the birth of Mithras, but as a celebration of the birth of Christ...

Dexter goes on to explore the possible origin of Cornish saint-days, pointing out that nothing is known of the biography of St Wenep of Gwennap, but that her name, in Cornish, means 'white horse': *Gwennap Feast with its 'saint' Wenep is in origin a pagan festival of the White Horse. Saint Wenep is the pagan White Horse masquerading as a Christian saint, nothing more, nothing less.*

Most of the rest of the book draws on his knowledge of Cornish place-names in a similar way: *St Michael Penkevil means 'The Sun as represented by the Horse's Head'. There is no doubt that this Church is one of many on a pagan site, in this case a site of sun- and horse-worship.*

There is a lengthy exposition relating to Liskeard, and a number of other places: *The Welsh Kerridwen was among other things a moon goddess. The Cornish Kerid seems also to have been one for her fair at Liskeard (Lis-kerid means 'Kerids Court') is on the eve of the autumnal equinox, which was originally a moon date...*

Din-sul 'Sun-hill' is said by a medieval commentator to be an old name for St Michaels Mount....there is much in favour of the ideas that St Michael is the successor of the sun-god and that St Michaels Mount was once a place of sun-worship...

40

St Ewe is a Christianisation of the (Sun) god Hu (Ew-e) and the connecting link between the saint and the god would seem to be the feast day Nov 1st samhain a thoroughly pagan date.... St Cury seems the (Irish) pagan sun-god Curoi in the thinnest of disguises...

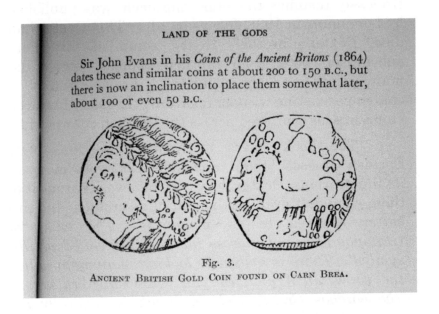

LAND OF THE GODS

Sir John Evans in his *Coins of the Ancient Britons* (1864) dates these and similar coins at about 200 to 150 B.C., but there is now an inclination to place them somewhat later, about 100 or even 50 B.C.

Fig. 3.

ANCIENT BRITISH GOLD COIN FOUND ON CARN BREA.

In 'Land of the Gods' TFG Dexter suggests the horse on the reverse of this coin found on Carn Brea has the head of a chicken and the legs of a greyhound, and is therefore a representation of Kerid, the pagan goddess associated with Liskeard in North Cornwall.

Dexter takes a swipe at Jenner and Morton-Nance, leaders of the Cornish revival who, like a number of his peers, were sceptical of his theories: *In this hour of reaction towards (ie revival of) medievalism, the man who dares to hint at a doubt concerning any one of the Cornish saints becomes according to the devotees of a certain school of thought an outcast fit only for the society of heretics, cranks and other impossible people.*

'Cornish Crosses - Christian and Pagan', which tirelessly resumes the same approach, was published by Longmans in 1938, five years after TFG Dexter had died. Dexter's brother, Henry, compiled this more substantial book from brother Thomas' notes and manuscripts, and the result is a brave attempt to challenge existing wisdom regarding the many hundred stone crosses scattered across the Cornish countryside.

The book refers to Arthur Langdon's 'Old Cornish Crosses' (1896), and indeed borrows many of its illustrations. Dexter, however, believes that most of them shouldn't even be thought of as crosses, and are better referred to as 'monoliths': *The cross at Grampound is not a cross but a thinly-veiled phallic symbol'....There is a strange looking monument called the Crowz-an-Wra in Buryan. Crowz-an-Wra means 'the witches Cross', and the witch is generally the successor of the pagan priestess; perchance we have in the name, a folk memory of pagan rites once celebrated at this monolith, the head of which forms a crude wheel: a Sun-symbol. The common people have thus preserved the memory that some crosses are pagan that is to say folklore and folk custom in Cornwall tell us something which many connoisseurs of Cornwall have forgotten or are unwilling to know, namely that all Cornish crosses are not necessarily Christian.*

Dexter points out that crosses were used as symbols for many hundreds of years before

Christianity. The Greek cross symbolised the four directions of space, whilst for the Chaldo Assyrians, it was a symbol of the sun. Many other cultures used a four-spoked wheel as a sun-symbol, *the wheel probably represented the radiant progressing power of the sun'*, and according to Dexter many such cultures used imitative magic (eg using flaming wheels) in a magical attempt to make the sun brighter and more vigorous.

Dexter, referring to Langdon, identifies fifty wheel crosses in Cornwall, some of which have slanting spokes, and some a central boss representing the axle of the wheel. In fact, Dexter identifies no less than 7 crosses indicating sun-worship in the village of Lanivet alone, and comments that the name itself perhaps derives from the word Lan-eu-et meaning enclosure of Hu (a sun god identified in Welsh literature by Iolo Morgawng).

Whilst Dexter's comments on wheel crosses have some credibility, much of the rest of the book is interesting but more speculative. For example, in looking for traces of pagan religious practice, Dexter identifies two crosses bearing images of men with tails (in Morrab Gardens and Lanivet churchyard) suggesting, that they might have been *'worn for ceremonial purposes'*.

He also restates the contention first introduced in 'Civilisation in Britain' that some forty Cornish crosses are based on Egyptian ankhs, a symbol of the key of life: *'it will be noted that they are found chiefly in the metalliferous areas - an indication but not a proof of a possible connection between the Ankh and metals,*

43

the link being the Eastern metal seekers who brought the Ankh with them.

Dexter anticipates post-war alternative archaeology in equating St Uny or Uni with Juno the Earth Mother or Earth Goddess and refers to the fogou at Chapel Uny thus: *'the more we investigate the subject the more we are forced to the conclusion that the fogou at Chapel Uny was designed for the worship of the Earth Mother, and the Earth Mother revered there was Uni, whom we have found as an Etruscan goddess'.*

He points out that none of the crosses depicting a human figure clearly indicate a crucifixion, and instead they are, perhaps, humanized (or anthropomorphized) ankhs.

Finally, he notes that according to Langdon 27% round headed crosses in Cornwall are damaged, compared with only 8% of the Latin ones. This would fit with them being pagan monuments. Dexter also points out how the early church tried to suppress 'stone-worship'. *'Christianity in Cornwall grew up (or was evolved) in a pagan environment and in growing up it absorbed much paganism; all this is gall and wormwood to some Cornish archaeologists today, unwilling as they are to admit the influence of paganism on the early Christianity of Cornwall; so they keep or try to keep their Christianity in a water-tight compartment. If at all possible, folklore and folk custom are given a Christian explanation: if an explanation along Christian lines be impossible, then the subject is disregarded or neglected'.*

Sadly, though the much-loved Doreen Valiente quotes from his Fire Festivals books, TFG Dexter's ideas have remained something of an obscure footnote. He was, however, ahead of his time and I would suggest is deserving of a reappraisal.

References (works by Dexter cited in the text)

Dexter, T.F.G. and Garlick, A.H. (1902) *Psychology In The Schoolroom,* Longmans Green and Co, London

Dexter, T.F.G. (1926) *Cornish Names - An Attempt to Explain over 1600 Cornish Names* (republished as Cornish Names) London; Longmans Green and Co

Dexter T.F.G. (undated) *Civilisation In Britain 2000 B.C.* New Knowledge Press, Perranporth, Cornwall

Dexter, T. F. G. (undated) *The Pagan Origin of Fairs.* New Knowledge Press, Perranporth, Cornwall

T.F.G. Dexter (1929) *The Sacred Stone.* New Knowledge Press, Treberran, Perranporth, Cornwall

Dexter, T.F.G. (1931) *Fire Worship in Britain* [New Knowledge Series No. 4] Watts & Co, London, United Kingdom

Dexter T.F.G. (1932) *Cornwall: The Land Of The Gods.* Jordan's Bookshop, Truro Cornwall, 1932

Dexter, T.F.G. (1933) *A Pre-History Reader or History from Things not Books. (World of Youth Library No. 14)* Watts, London

Dexter, T.F.G & Dexter, Henry (1938) *Cornish Crosses - Christian and Pagan* London; Longmans Green & Co.

St. Keyne's Well

Robert Charles Hope

This well is half a mile east of the interesting Decorated and Perpendicular Church of the same name, 2 ½ miles on the road from West Looe. It is a spring of rare virtues in the belief of the country people. It is covered in by masonry, upon the top of which formerly grew five large trees - a Cornish elm, an oak, and three antique ash trees - on so narrow a space that it is difficult to imagine how the roots could have been accommodated. There now remain only two of these trees; the elm, which is large  and fine, and one of the ash trees. According to the legend, St. Keyne, a holy and beautiful virgin, of British royal blood, daughter of Braganus, Prince of Brecknockshire, said to have been the aunt of St. David of Wales, visited this country about 490. She was sought in marriage by [15] men of distinction. On a pilgrimage to St. Michael's Mount, and remaining sometime in Cornwall, she so endeared herself to the people, that she was hardly allowed to depart. Her nephew, St. Cadock, making a pilgrimage to the same place, in surprise found her, and tried to persuade her to return to Brecknockshire, which eventually she did. Cadock stuck his stick in the earth, and originated the spring, which St. Keyne gave to the people in return for the church) which they had dedicated in her honour. One of her fancies was to reside in a wood at Keynsham. The chief of the country warned her of the venomous serpents which swarmed the wood. St. Keyne answered that she would by her prayers rid the country of snakes, and they were turned into the ammonites, frequently found in the lias rock in that district. The well is said to share with St. Michael's Chair at the Mount the marvellous property of confirming the ascendancy of either husband or wife who, the

ST. KEYNE.

first after marriage, can obtain a draught of water from the spring, or be seated in the chair.

Text and second illustration from the Legendary Lore of the Holy Wells of England. First illustration is from the 1936 Legends of Britain Churchman's cigarette card series.

Gwithti an Pystri

A Cabinet of Folklore and Magic

A report on Steve Patterson's pop-up exhibition, which ran during Summer 2021 in Falmouth, by Alex Langstone.

I recently took time to visit a brand-new pop-up exhibition. Titled *The Museum of Magic and Folklore*, this latest project by folklorist and antiquarian Steve Patterson can be found deep within the old vaults of Falmouth's Cornish Bank in Church Street.

As you enter this mysterious cavernous world, you are greeted with images and idols of Cornish folklore: Crying the Neck, Midsummer fires, Penglaz, Kasek Nos, Helston Furry and Padstow Obby Oss all vie for your attention, as they creep and sidle up to you. However, as you become accustomed to the rich and thick atmospheres of this folkloric world of wonder, an even more unusual item draws you inwards. For here sits Tim Shaw's fascinating and unexpected sculpture of the Obby Oss in front of the Crucifixion. Inspired by the artist's observation in 2011, which saw the Oss dancing before the high altar in St Petroc's parish church. This deeply inspired Shaw and led to the creation of this strange and somewhat unusual bronze sculpture of the iconic Padstow Oss.

Upon entering the main vault, the lighting changes and a deliciously eerie ambient soundtrack entices you to submit into a world of sea monsters, witches, and magic. Here is a world of mystery and enchantment, illustrated with artefacts from practitioners of witchery old and new, including Cecil Williamson's Witch's Cradle, many items from the art of the sea witch, a tableau of the sorcerer's lair and many other artefacts of Cornish and West Country traditional practice.

As you leave the museum, you may notice a cabinet of pisky lore and magic. Piskies are the Cornish branch of the faery tribe of the Isle of Britain. Containing charms and idols of the Cornish little folk, including a four leaved clover, a hag stone charm and brass images of Joan the Wad and Jack O Lantern.

It is difficult not to compare this small and intimate collection with the larger and established Museum of Witchcraft & Magic in Boscastle. Both collections are outstanding, but Steve's very personal and intimate collection, under the streets of the bustling maritime port of Falmouth, uncovers a deliciously eerie glimpse into the world of folklore which feels like it may have actually emerged from the sea and soil that surrounds it's subterranean lair.

These vaults below the old Cornish Bank lie close to the waterfront and contain a mysterious tunnel. What a perfect space to house these esoteric and folkloric items of magic and sorcery. This collection is an interesting glimpse into the world of enchantment, and one I would highly recommend.

The exhibition is now closed, but Steve is planning to relaunch the museum under its new name *"Gwithti an Pystri – a cabinet of folklore and magic"* and will reopen at a new location in Falmouth at Easter 2022.

Pisky cabinet of curiosities, as displayed during the Summer of 2021 at Falmouth's temporary Museum of magic and folklore.

Industrial Drolls:
The Sub-Genre of the 'Cousin-Jack Story' in Cornish Folklore

Alan M. Kent

This article posits an argument that so-called 'Cousin-Jack Stories' are a sub-genre of oral narrative from Cornwall. The stories are most associated with Cornish miners and their wives overseas (Cousin Jacks and Jennies), and although they are displaced narratives, they at least partially embody a tradition of earlier oral narrative that has been collected and anthologised in Cornwall. The 'Cousin-Jack Story' almost precisely matches the rise and fall of Cornish emigration overseas, with its heyday being the opening decades of the twentieth century. Since the end of the twentieth century, much of the traditional corpus is still known (particularly in North America), but as a whole, it has declined in line with the rest of the post-industrial world that the Cornish find themselves a part of.

Put simply, these industrial drolls were often in the form of advice to younger miners about the best way to conduct oneself, though occasionally, they also deal with wider issues and reiterate stereotypical images of Cornish identity and Anglo-Cornish dialect. This may be deemed appropriate, since in general, this was Cornish-generated humour. As several readers know, I first began to study 'Cousin-Jack Stories' in an article in 2004,[35] though since then I have found a number of other sources and stories. There is not the space here to consider all of the progress made but some samples and a commentary may provide the reader with an introduction to the sub-genre, which it is hoped, will prompt further enquiry.

Most studies of Cornish emigration tend to focus exclusively on statistics, so-called 'push-and-pull factors of migration, and the lasting effects of that migration on particular countries or territories.[36] Considerable time in Cornish Studies also has been spent documenting the more obvious territories to which Cornish people migrated; among them the United States of America, Australia, Mexico and South Africa. So far, rather less time, with a few notable exceptions, has been devoted to considering places such as Canada, New Zealand, India and Zimbabwe where there was also a major Cornish presence. Theories of emigration, the documentation of specific families, as well as technical detail and the migrant Cornish today has tended to dominate the field.

Over the course of time, we have tended to see less studies of the cultural impact of such migration, the organic folklore that went along with this migration and the literature that was generated from it. However, both I myself and a number of other scholars have tried

---

[35] Alan M. Kent, "Drill-Cores': A Newly-Found Manuscript of Cousin-Jack Narratives from the Upper Peninsula of Michigan, USA' in Philip Payton (ed.), Cornish Studies: Twelve, Exeter: University of Exeter Press, 2004, pp.106-143.
[36] In its most popular form, this is seen in volumes such as Philip Payton, The Cornish Overseas, Fowey: Alexander Associates, 1999.

hard in recent years, to redress this imbalance.[37] It may well be that the outward information about Cornish migration is easier to map (shipping lists, employee records and physical remains in the landscape), whereas culture, folklore and literature require a little deeper digging. They are less obvious and sometimes more ephemeral. Folklore and literature can soon be forgotten, whereas all Cornish communities around the world leave remnants of their material culture: engine houses, stacks, smelters and so on.

Many readers here will not have encountered Cousin-Jack Stories before. They are aware of what Cousin Jacks are, but identifying and mapping a range of stories written by them and about them may be rather more difficult. Compared to the almost limitless expansion of Cornish and Anglo-Cornish

[37] The earliest of these studies was Hadley Tremaine, 'Cornish Folk Speech in America', in Midwestern Journal of Language and Folklore, Terre Haute: Indiana State University, Volume VI , No. 2, 1980, pp.17-25. See also Alan M. Kent, '"Mozeying on Down...": The Cornish Language in America' in Hildeguard L. C, Tristram (ed.), The Celtic Languages in Contact, Potsdam: Potsdam University Press, 2007, pp.193-217; Alan M. Kent and Gage McKinney (eds.), The Busy Earth: A Reader in Global Cornish Literature 1700-2000, St Austell: Cornish Hillside Publications, 2008.

Literature (by both indigenous and non-indigenous authors), Cousin-Jack Stories occupy a small sub-genre within that field, and may perhaps be categorised under what Cornish people like to call 'Dialect' but, in fact, is much more accurately described as Cornu-English. They can be labelled Cornu-English but at the same time, they are not truly Cornu-English because they have been infused with the language of the countries and territories that they emerged in. As Hickey neatly puts it, they are a 'legacy of Colonial English' and also examples of 'transported dialects'.[38] These dialects, however, remain powerful marks of identity both during the golden age of their circulation but also form a lightning rod for us in the here and now, connecting past and present.

I first became interested in Cousin-Jack Stories during a succession of travels I made to Cornish migration 'hotspots' during the opening decade of the twenty-first century.[39] These were initially in the United States of America and Mexico, but also in Australia and New Zealand. Visiting epi-centres of Cornishness, I discovered that this sub-genre of folklore and of literature still existed, and it intrigued me, for in them it seemed were perfect examples of transnational Cornishness, coupled with the fact, that however distant they were from 'home', they retained an essence of not only Cornu-English but also of a resolutely Cornish ideology and humour about life. If we are to say

---

[38] Raymond Hickey (ed.), Legacies of Colonial English: Studies in Transported Dialects, Cambridge: Cambridge University Press, 2004. For a wider context on this, see Tony Capstick, Language and Migration, London: Routledge, 2020.
[39] See Alan M, Kent, Cousin-Jack's Mouth-Organ: Travels in Cornish America, St Austell: Cornish Hillside Publications, 2004.

that Cornu-English, even in the late nineteenth century was infused by some of the language, rhythm and constructions of Cornish itself, then we may also find vestigial remains of this in such tales. To me, this legacy was irresistibly fascinating, and I was instantly drawn to them. They reminded me of the kinds of tales I was told to me as a youngster by my granfer and great-uncle in woodsheds and workshops of mid-Cornwall in the 1970s. A somewhat typical example may be found in this piece from 1940 committed to print by Charles E. Brown:

A Cornish miner was trudging to town with a bag over his shoulder to buy some supplies. In walking past the home of a settler he was suddenly set upon by a dog who growled and showed his teeth. While he was trying to defend himself against Towser by swinging the bag about, the owner of the dog called out. "Jack, that dorg won't bite, 'e's waggin' 'es tail!" "I knoaw that," replied Cousin Jack. "E's waggin' 'es tail at one h'end and barkin' at the other. I doan't naw which of 'es heads to believe."[40]

Sometimes, mention of Cousin-Jack Stories were somewhat vague, though when say, I delved into the cartoons of Oswald Pryor from Australia,[41] I learnt that underneath the wit found in those sketches of mining, Cap'ns and Billy Goat-pulled wagons was something

---

[40] Charles E. Brown, Cousin Jack Stories: Short Stories of the Cornish Lead Mines in South-western Wisconsin, Madison: Wisconsin Folklore Society, 1940, p.2
[41] Oswald Pryor, Cousin Jack Cartoons, Sydney and Melborne: Frank Johnson, 1945, Cornish Pasty: A Book of Cartoons, Adelaide: Rigby, 1960 [1950], Cousin Jacks and Jennies, Adelaide: Rigby, 1966.

called the Cousin-Jack Story. It soon became obvious that these were a set of comic, industrial narratives which considered the Cornish overseas and documented their daily lives and struggles.

They were very different to the kind of emigration studies I had read when I was younger, which seemed to more technical, economic and geographical-based. In them, it was clear that culture (in all its forms and varieties; sometimes tasteful, sometimes not) was going to be depicted. It was also clear that these stories had a specific context for telling; that they had a storytelling moment in the societies in which they emerged: sometimes this was during crib or crowst time; more often in bars or saloons that the Cornish frequented, but also in the boarding houses and bunk-houses of the mining frontiers, in order to pass time through the long winter nights; this one from c.1947 by the shadowy Cousin Jan:

A fellow was standing in front of the dime store one morning after the night shift. Down the Library hill came his partner, pretty much in a hurry. The fellow in front of the dime store said. "Old fast, 'Arry, where you going? What's your 'urry?" Said the other fellow, "I'm over to the 'ospital." "What say?" "My missus ed'n looking good. I'm going over and get a drop of medicine." "Old on, boy. I'll go with 'ee. I don't like the looks of mine either."[42]

However, in studying the stories, it was also clear to me that they had sometimes a very specific mentoring purpose: that their tellings by older, more experienced miners, had an educative effect on younger miners, and that their narratives were in effect, coded warnings and advice on how to behave, and how not behave. These were sometimes stories that could save your life and keep you safe. This behaviour was both that found underground and in the mining context above ground but also about the communities they were 'shoved into', where they had ended-up. Therefore, the kind of language associated with many of the tales ('M'son' or 'M'lad') seemed to suggest older wisdom being passed on. Thus, the stories extended beyond mining life, to other experiences such as relationships,

---

[42] From Cousin Jan MS. Copy held in the editor's collection. For a useful fictional depiction of this culture, see s Newton G. Thomas, The Long Winter Ends, New York: The Macmillan Company, 1941.

marriage, money, hunting, sport, pastimes and most of all, modern Cornish identity.

The exact origin of Cousin-Jack Stories is something I have much contemplated, but I cannot offer a true answer to their emergence. The first recorded story I offer here comes from the latter end of the nineteenth century, and the date of 1875 is still comparatively early. It was written anonymously and published in a newspaper called the *Territorial Enterprise*. It seems that, even by this date, observers had expectations about Cornish behaviours; in this particular case, the way they characteristically used aspirated vowel sounds in their speech:

A Cornishman asked an American if he could guess the three fruits in his lunch pail, all of which began with the letter 'h..' The American could not guess, so the Cornishman revealed that they were 'a h'apple, a h'orange, and a h'apricot'. [43]

It suggests however, that the basis of a Cousin-Jack Story had already crossed to Nevada in the west of the United States of America, and as we know, and many historians have documented, the history of the Cornish in that country has tended to move from east to west.[44] Therefore, if the earliest story is from this year, then surely they would have been told much

---

[43] From Territorial Enterprise, c.1875. My thanks to Ronald M. James for making me aware of this text.
[44] The classic studies are A. C. Todd, The Cornish Miner in America, Truro: D. Bradford Barton, 1967; A. L. Rowse, The Cornish in America, Redruth; Dyllansow Truran, 1991 [1969]; John Rowe, The Hard Rock Men: Cornish Immigrants on the North American Mining Frontier, Liverpool: Liverpool University Press, 1974.

earlier on, and in places both in the north of the country (Wisconsin and Michigan) and in the east (Virginia and Pennsylvania), where Cornishmen and women first worked. This supposition suggests in fact, that by 1875 stories about Cousin Jacks told by others and Cousin Jacks inventing stories about themselves were already well established. The ethnic group was understood, and people understood who the Cousin Jacks were. They were different; something that flies in the face of the Cornish in such territories simply being regarded as English.

What is puzzling, however, is that the sub-genre was not that well-established in Cornwall itself. It is hard to find comparable narratives in the hefty canon of folklore from Cornwall. Nowhere in the great folklore collectors' work (in texts such as those of Hunt, Bottrell and Courtney[45]) do we find embryonic forms of the Cousin-Jack Story. It seems therefore that the sub-genre arose overseas alone and that it was trans-nationality that prompted their telling. As well as them acting as mentoring devices, they therefore were also a way of maintaining Cornish identity, and in so doing not being afraid of self-deprecation and poking fun at

---

[45] Robert Hunt, Popular Romances of the West of England: The Drolls, Traditions, and Superstitions of Old Cornwall (First Series), London: John Camden Hotton, 1865, Popular Romances of the West of England: The Drolls: Traditions, and Superstitions of Old Cornwall (Second Series), London: John Camden Hotten, 1865; William Bottrell, Traditions and Hearthside Stories of West Cornwall: First Series, Penzance: W. Cornish, 1870, Traditions and Hearthside Stories of West Cornwall, Second Series, Penzance: Beare and Son, 1873, Traditions and Hearthside Stories of West Cornwall: Third Series, Penzance: F. Rodda, 1880; M. A. Courtney, Folklore and Legends of Cornwall [Cornish Feasts and Feasten Customs], Exeter: Cornwall Books, 1989 [1890].

their own ways of operating. This is seen in the following example by Walter F. Gries, recorded in 1959:

In our underground mines in Northern Michigan there was a new program developed 'in the 1940s. Instead of the miners eating their 'crib'—or their lunch—at their working place, dining rooms with tables and lights were built underground. Miners can wash their hands and take their lunch buckets to the tables. A young Cornishman came in with the boys at crib time, put his lunch bucket up on the table, opened it up, took out a thermos bottle of tea and began to unwrap his sandwiches. He looked at the sandwiches and said, "Look 'ere! Peanut butter sandwiches! 'Ow can a man do h'any minin' on peanut butter san'wiches?"

Nobody paid any attention to him. The next day, the same thing happened. "Look! There they are h'again! Peanut butter san'wiches! H'I 'avn 'ad no pasty in two weeks!" Nobody paid any attention. The third day—the same routine. Finally, one of his partners spoke up. "W'y dawn't 'ee say somethin' to y're missus about it?" "Naow look e ere," said the young miner, "you leave my missus aout o' this! H'I put they h'up myself."[46]

[46] Donald D. Kinsey (ed.), Drill Cores: Folklore of Michigan's Upper Peninsula, from the Collection of Walter F. Gries, MS., c.1959, p.82.

In the mix that was expanding America, the tales and their language retained a link to home. Their telling told the Cornish who they were and where they had come from. The lack of a link is most curious, and I still have no explanation for it. It is not enough to say they are connected to the mining narratives found in Hunt and Bottrell. The recent work of James has been crucial in documenting the origins, passage and retelling of Cornish folklore over the centuries,[47] though it does seem that in the continuum, the Cousin-Jack Story is a comparative late arrival. The term I use here to consider this kind of narrative, and indeed, the title of this article: Industrial Drolls' seems apt, however.

These are the drolls from the industrial period. The earlier folklore was, for the most part (bar some mining stories) pre-industrial. As Jenner suggests, that the Cornish-language word *daralla* lead into the Cornu-

[47] Ronald M. James, The Folklore of Cornwall: The Oral Tradition of a Celtic Nation, Exeter: University of Exeter Press, 2019.

English word 'droll',[48] then we begin to gain a good understanding of how these tales work. They are indeed drolls and *droll* is the word that generations of Cornish people used to label stories; hence the term 'droll-teller'. Cousin-Jack Stories may therefore be confidently termed industrial drolls for they represent a new phase of storytelling during the industrial age.

There are alternative views on this, however. McMahon has articulated that the final phases of folklore collecting happened in Cornwall just as industry became more intense.[49] Thus, folklore collection by those great folklorists like Hunt, Bottrell and Courtney were almost a Romantic-period reaction to the fact, that if they did not act, then the canon of material would be forever lost, because people would stop their telling. Their collection had two effects: it did preserve the canon in perhaps a more comprehensive way than on any other equivalent part of these islands, yet it also encoded and fossilized the stories preventing their further development.[50] This is, of course, one of the most fundamental debates about folklore. The collection restricts growth but preservation from complete loss is the better option.

---

[48]Henry Jenner, 'Some Possible Arthurian Place-Names in West Penwith' in Journal of the Royal Institution of Cornwall, 1912, p.87. Richard Gendall also defines the word daralla as 'story, tale, droll, account, legend, information, report, report of conditions'. See Richard Gendall (ed.), A Practical Dictionary of Modern Cornish, Menheniot: Teere ha Tavaz, 1997, p.35.

[49] Brendan McMahon, A Wreck on the Ocean: Cornish Folklore in the Age of the Industrial Revolution, Portlaoise: Evertype, 2015.

[50] Alan M. Kent, The Literature of Cornwall: Continuity, Identity, Difference 1000-2000, Bristol: Redcliffe, 2000, pp.124-30.

McMahon also contends that storytelling is an act of 'cultural resistance',[51] and this seems a very valid model to apply onto the Cousin-Jack Stories. Although the great age of folklore collecting was over, ironically these Stories emerge in a period when they were not meant to. Industrialism was meant to confound and prevent stories from emerging, but this was not the case with the Cornish, and if we regard emigration as the next stage in Cornish people's cultural and economic development, then it seems convincing that a new genre of storytelling was likely to emerge. This was the Cousin-Jack Story. This supports a view I first suggested back in 2000 that the Cornish were different than other Celtic nations (most obviously the agrarian and environmentally- 'green' model of Celticity offered in particular by territories such as Ireland) and that they were 'industrial Celts'.[52] This conceptualisation of Cornishness is one of the reasons (alongside the revitalization of the Cornish language) why it took so long for the Cornish to be accepted as Celtic. For a while, it seemed liked you could not be truly Celtic if you were industrial. Nonetheless, the Cousin-Jack Story has maintained continuity through the industrial period, and is still being told in the post-industrial age, albeit on a smaller scale.

---

[51] Brendan McMahon, Gathering the Fragments: Storytelling and Cultural Resistance in Cornwall, Portlaoise: Evertype, 2016.

[52] Kent, op.cit. p.124. This agrarian view is supported in texts such as Gracie Clunue and Tess Maginess, The Celtic Spirit and Literature, Dunlin: The Columba Press, who find industrialisation an anathema to Celticity. See also, Bernard Deacon, Industrial Celts: Making the Modern Cornish Identity 1750-1870, Redruth: Cornish Social and Economic Research Group, 2018.

Consider this story called 'Long in the Saddle' by Walter F. Gries from 1959:[53]

These days, m'son, h'everything is for h'increased capacity. Moore tons per man, larger skips, bigger cars—an' so h'it gaws till it saym as though, h'outside of timberin' like we did in the h'early days minen was sort o' lily-putian back then. But jus' the same, m'son, 'twasn't as though we dedn' ave some notion to make the most o' wot we 'ad. I remember one time, years h'ago in Grass Valley, Jimmy Trebilock went to the livery stable and sez, "Gimme the best 'ole 'orse thee's got h'in the stable. H'I'm gawin to a gert dance tonight." "Thee dosn't want a 'orse, thee wants a 'orse an' buggy," sez the owner. "Gos along, do, sez Jimmy, "dawn't thee tell me w'at I want. H'I wants a orse weth a bloody long back. There's five o' us goin'."

Trying to map the stories with the sub-genre has been difficult. I tried my best to work in historical order, though sometimes this has not always been possible. There are sometimes later variants of earlier stories which are better, and more comprehensive. There are also probably earlier variants of later stories which have fallen by the way. There is a considerable jump between the acknowledged first extant story (found in 1875) and those being collected in 1920. Maybe some of those early stories were not passed down or were not written down. Maybe they were written down but

---

[53] Donald D. Kinsey (ed.), Drill Cores: Folklore of Michigan's Upper Peninsula, from the Collection of Walter F. Gries, MS., c.1959, p.86.

rather sadly, have simply been lost. All of this reminds me of what I have often said about literature in Cornish. It is silly to wail about the considerable texts that have been lost. It is better to consider the weight and wonder of the texts that have survived and that are still with us. The same premise can surely be applied onto Cousin-Jack Stories.

In 2008 Gage McKinney and I made a stab at collating as much global Cornish literature as we could trace into a single volume, including there, some Cousin-Jack Stories.[54] We were very much aware then that if we did not complete that task then, that many of the texts would probably never see the light of day, and languish in collections or libraries without readers really knowing what was written. In succeeding years, I have tried very hard to record and trace Cousin-Jack Stories from the Cornish overseas. Two fundamental and very sobering facts remain. The first is that almost exclusively the surviving canon is from the United States of America. I cannot account for why this is. Perhaps had I been operating some fifty years earlier; I would have discovered more across the globe. I am sure, for example, that many Cousin-Jack Stories were told in Australia, New Zealand and South Africa, but so far, I have been unable to locate them. Perhaps they may still reveal themselves (see below).

The second is that what I have located may well be (more or less) the entire sub-genre. It could indeed by the case that in such territories, the tales told in America were merely adapted elsewhere. This may well seem likely because in their lives Cornishmen and

---

[54] Kent and McKinney, op,cit.

women were incredibly mobile, with some families working first in one country, and then moving on to elsewhere; in fact, to wherever the work was plentiful. Perhaps then, the tales moved too. Certainly, there are moments in Pryor's cartoons of Australia which match moments in the stories from the United States of America. Curiously though, I cannot find a single story that matches anything I have heard or seen at home in Cornwall; perhaps another point proving the stories overseas' individuality.

As the reader has seen in the 1875 story above, one of the markers of Cornishness is the Cousin Jack's use of aspirated vowels. I do not know how I feel about this. Is it a well-intentioned depiction of Cornu-English speech or is there something more derogatory about it, suggesting that such pretention is the marker of the stupidity of the Cornish? We shall

probably never know. It does, however, seem to be, that by the time that some of the classic Cousin-Jack Stories had been formulated then this way of speaking was encoded into the stories, and was a marker of Cousin-Jack speech, clearly identifiable to a listening audience. I cannot say it is not a true marker of Cornu-English speech because I can go to any meeting of say, a local town council or an Old Cornwall Society and hear it there. Thankfully, thanks to observers such as Sandow, the socio-linguistics of Cornu-English is becoming more and more understood and given full academic treatment.[55]

As yet, I do not have information about all of the recorders and tellers of Cousin-Jack Stories. Sometimes, my dating of the stories is based on a triangulation of lots of different sources which lead me to think they were written down in a particular time period. However, we know that the date of their recording is a good deal later than their date of composition or circulation. On the whole, I always estimate this to be perhaps at least some quarter of a century after they were first told. Documenting precise differences, amendments, transition in characterisation and speech patterns might be a task for someone to complete in the future, but that is not my purpose here.

Like all storytelling cultures that have ever existed, one imagines a whole set of 'Chinese whispers' taking place across the Cornish Diaspora which has sometimes retained elements of stories, sometimes redacted elements and sometimes embroidered them

---

[55] See Rhys J. Sandow, Anglo-Cornish Dialect Lexis: Variation, Change and Social Meaning, Ph.D thesis, University of Sussex, 2020, 'The Anglo-Cornish Dialect is 'a performance, a deliberate performance' in English Today, Volume 36, Special Issue 3, 2020, pp.77-84.

further. By twenty-first century standards, some of the stories are, in some ways, disturbing or unpleasant. Working the mining frontiers around the world was often disturbing and unpleasant. Some of the stories are environmentally unfriendly (they involved hunting, the mistreatment of animals and the exploitation of the natural landscape) but the environmental movement is a recent thing, and perhaps far from these tellers' minds when they were first orated. Likewise, the treatment of women is not always very nice but having said that, men who act badly often get their comeuppance. We still do not know enough whether Cousin Jennies also partook in such tellings. I suspect they did, although the times and the places of those tellings are less well documented.

So, I have found, the tellers, the recorders and the subject are shape-shifters. Presumably, names were rendered differently for each telling, and places were swapped to give them more local relevance and resonance. The reader will sometimes note that stories are often set just outside of the local area, or beyond it, in a place that is well enough known, but not so that it would offend anyone in the immediate telling. The culture of storytelling seems to have varied from being within the levels and stopes of the mine, to the grass-side workings and to places such as bars, saloons and barbers (overtly 'male' space). One imagines that a telling of one story often resulted in another even better story being told, and in several of the tales, that culture is depicted.

In the classic era of Cousin-Jack storytelling, perhaps between 1900 and 1930, globally, there were probably hundreds of tellers who could articulate the kinds of drolls examined here. In some communities the stories were known as drolls. In others they were called tales or yarns. In some others, they were called 'plods'. This latter description is interesting for it assumes a certain predictable quality to the telling: that the story plodded along, until the punch-line. Perhaps however, the term plod denies the sophistication of some of the narrative, and their placing of the necessary elements to make the story work. The punch-line usually does arrive in a piece of well-observed and pointed observation, but its impact has usually been determined by the placing of an earlier element which sometimes the reader or listener may initially have not paid enough attention to. In many stories I often note Cornish anti-logic. This term is not intended to be derogatory. It just a term that seems to summarise Cornish ideology when dealing with certain situations. In this sense, it seems to defy conventional logic, but somehow is remarkably Cornish in the way that it sees the world. It is in this way that Cornish identity comes across.

Sometimes, the difference between a teller and a recorder is hard to note. Very often tellers were not concerned with documentation, but recorders certainly saw something original in the tales and so began to document them. An early teller such as D. E. A. Chorlton probably had more stories to tell, but only a few it seems, were published. Chorlton does not document his sources, but then again, he may well be an original teller himself. He tended to concentrate on poetry; material that is already documented in Kent and McKinney's volume.[56] Charles E. Brown was a substantial collector, and his published collection was an important volume in terms of establishing the genre. His stories though, are relatively short and contain less Cornu-English. This dialect somehow gets a little lost in transmission from mouth to page. Ernie Hocking was clearly an important teller in Grass Valley in California but despite my best affords, I have found no other tales beyond the ones contained here. With him it is again a case of wondering 'If only...'

The greatest teller and recorder remains Walter F. Gries (1892-1959), whose life and work I comprehensively documented in the article published in 2004.[57] I do not wish to revisit that here, and so the reader is urged to consult that material for further detail on Gries. This is not to deny the importance of Donald D. Kinsey (c.1902-1965) who helped to later compile Gries' stories. Kinsey organised and developed the so-called *Drill-Cores* manuscript into a kind of 'play' format, where there were a cast of characters who were the Cousin Jacks and Jennies of the Upper Peninsula of Michigan and who had their tales to tell. Like a modern-day Geoffrey Chaucer, Kinsey devised a frame for Gries' tellers and their tales.

However, since this time, I have also been passed an earlier Gries manuscript which here forms the basis of what I term the Cousin Jan narratives. This manuscript pre-dates *Drill-Cores* and seems to have been imagined by Gries working often overtly as 'Cousin Jan'. Perhaps he was aware that his surname

---

[56] Kent and McKinney, op,cit.
[57] Kent, in Philip (ed.), 2004, pp.106-143.

was not Cornish. As I outlined in the 2004 article, it was to my great disappointment that I was unable to meet William 'Jack' Foster who died in 2003 (a year before I started seriously working on the matter) and he was, supposedly, one of the great Cousin-Jack storytellers. I have since made investigation as to whether Jack Foster wrote down any of his stories but so far, I have not come across a manuscript or notebook. I do, however, live in hope, that somewhere his work will have been preserved. The likelihood of course, is that many of these mid-twentieth-century tellers all knew each other and specialised in particular tales. The details of that have, however, been lost.

I was fortunate enough in 2004 to hear one of the surviving and previously undocumented Cousin-Jack Stories told to me by Tom Ellis Jr. (with contributions from Phil Medlyn). This is given below:

There was Cousin Jack by the name of Alfie Elliot. He was a handyman who rented out boats on Lake Mosquito. That' a real lake mind—just over the way there. My wife's father used to rent boats off him— but only the beat-up, unpainted ones. One day Mrs Elliot came down to the shore, and sat right on one of the freshly-painted boats. So, my father-in-law piped up. "Alfie, your wife's sittin' on one of the boats."

"Er is," said Alfie. "Alfie, you knaw the paint's wet dun't ee?" "Ess," said Alfie. "Er'll knaw ut when she gets up..."[58]

---

[58] Kent, in Philip (ed.), 2004, pp.106-143.

I was very much aware that I was listening to the very last of a dying breed and I vowed then to make sure that the genre was documented and would not fall into complete extinction. Walter F. Gries was Tom Ellis Jr.'s grandfather so it was then possible to identify a lineage of tellers. Gries' father himself was one John Adams Gries, who lived and worked amongst the Cornish, and it was likely that he was the one who installed love of stories in his son. Amusingly, John Adams Gries, was known locally as 'Axle Gries', a name given to him almost from out of one of the stories. Thus, there is a lineage of telling beginning in the present with Tom Ellis Jr., his father Tom Ellis, his grandfather Walter F. Gries and eventually back to his great-grandfather John Adams Gries. Maybe it was John Adams Gries who was a partial instigator of the form and certainly an original teller. That we can trace this pattern of storytelling in four generations is incredible and shows the persistence of the sub-genre.

Compared to the corpus of work covered by Hunt, Bottrell and Courtney, as well as other folklorists who have come along in their wake,[59] the stories presented here may not seem much (they are not epic, nor involve battling against magical creatures or little people) but they are in this author's view just as important in documenting the lives of the Cornish as found in earlier generations. Happily, a new generation of scholars seems to be picking up on where the classic folklore collectors left off and are trying document and preserve

---

[59] One thinks here of recent contributors to Lien Gwerin: A Journal of Cornish Folklore. See Alex Langstone (ed.), Lien Gwerin: A Journal of Cornish Folklore, No.5, 2021, and the work of Kelvin L. Jones (ed.), The Cornish Folklore Collection, Volume One: Witchcraft, Spells, Cures and Superstitions, Liskeard: Oakmagic, 2020.

these narratives and pieces of folklore for future readers and tellers. It seems rather unlikely that there will ever be a full-scale revival of Cousin-Jack storytelling but on occasion, I have heard snippets and reminders from Cornish gatherings and festivals around the world that I have attended. Long may this continue, and hopefully this volume will re-ignite aspects of the corpus.[60] The symbol of the Cousin Jack shows no sign of slowing down, and hopefully their stories will not be lost either.

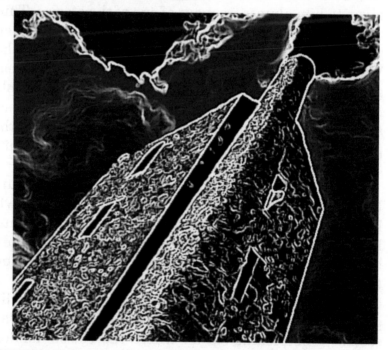

---

[60] As I was writing this article, I have become aware of the Timothy Tregonning narratives by the Australian writer Brian Medlin (1927-2004). The Timothy Tregonning narratives have a good many elements of earlier Cousin-Jack Stories. See Gillian Doolley, Wallace McKitrick and Susan Petralli (ed.), The Level-Headed Revolutionary: Essays, Stories and Poems by Brian Medlin, Mile End, South Australia: Wakefield Press, 2021.

Rambles and Ruminations

around the inner life of the Fogous of Cornwall

Steve Patterson

The idea of the empty cave/tomb is a spectre which haunts our myths and our dreams, and which also finds form in some of the enigmatic structures left for us by our prehistoric ancestors. One such example of this, of which there are a number of examples in Cornwall, is the Fogou. These prehistoric megalithic structures consist of a short stone lined tunnel about ten to twenty feet long, just below surface of the earth. The enigmatic Souterrain leads to nowhere but into itself, though folk belief often suggests that they are the beginning of a secret tunnel.

One example of this in the "Pisky's hall" Fogou in Constantine, which in local legend is said to be either the entrance to a tunnel to the adjacent Foxes Manor house or to a smugglers tunnel down to the Helford River some miles away. Surely to construct such a tunnel in secret would be an engineering near-impossibility! I strongly feel, that as with most secret tunnel stories, if such a secret tunnel does exist; it is not for the passage of the body but for the passing of the dreaming mind. Like the false doorways in the ancient Egyptian temples, these too seem to serve as an entrance into the intangible realm of our imagination. If any journeying is to be done, it is to pass within the confines of the fogou.

Their original purpose remains a mystery. None of them have yet yielded any funerary remains or ritual deposits to aid us in our speculations. One suggestion is that they were some kind of underground larder, but one cannot help but think that not only are they rather over built for such a mundane purpose, but they would also be a potential haven for vermin and rot.

Another equally implausible explanation is the idea that they were used as a hiding place in times of conflict, the low entrance causing the invaders to bump their heads if they attempted to enter; doubtlessly in turn causing the entire war band to fall over like dominoes! The authors of this hypothesis doubtlessly derived their knowledge of ancient military tactics from "Asterix the Gaul". Almost by default we are driven to a more esoteric conclusion.

I remember my first encounter with a fogou was in the 1980s when I met old Jo O'Cleirigh who lived in a wooden hut in the woods of Lamorna valley. One night we crept around the back of the manor house at the head of the Valley to the old Fogou that lay in its grounds. In the darkness of the garden behind the house we slipped down what seemed to be a portal formed of an even deeper darkness, and there we sat consumed in its earthy embrace, only the sound of our breath pierced the intense silence of the fogou. It was in this fogou that local legend told that the old lord of the manor, Squire Lovell, stumbled upon a coven of witches and there he heard the Devils secret name.

"Duffy and the devil" is a traditional Cornish droll collected by the folklorists Robert Hunt and William Bottrell in the mid-nineteenth century. The tale is almost a Cornish version of the more well-known Rumpelstiltskin story, but with the addition of a curiously inconclusive and pessimistic ending. Maybe this is indicative of the ambiguous and continually unexpected nature of the fogou itself.

Several years later on the eve of the devastating 1987 storms I was working on the trees near the Trelowarren Estate. I remember hammering in stakes from dawn till dusk until my hands locked into immobile claws. Each evening, using mugs of hot coffee, I would tease them back to life. One day an old estate worker told us of a cave above of fields in which we were working. On the last day of the job, we went to investigate. Battling through the undergrowth we found some steps going down to a subterranean entrance, later I was to discover this was Halliggye Fogou. As we entered my boss sternly warned me not to do any of my "weird pagan stuff" then inexplicably pulled a heavy brass candelabrum from his kit bag and lit the darkness. Once again I felt that familiar deep chthonic peace of the land permeate my being.

Since then, my encounters with the fogous of Cornwall have been many and varied. My closest acquaintance however has been with the fogous of the village of Constantine. I use the plural because there are indeed two; in addition to the well documented

"Pisky's hall" fogou is another hidden in the old overgrown Glebe Garden. I once mentioned this to the then Cornwall Archaeology unit, to which I was politely but firmly informed that there was no such fogou.

It is built in an identical manner to the Pisky's Hall, with straight dry stone walls and huge parallel recumbent slabs forming the roof. It disappears a short distance into a steep bank, terminating in a small chamber formed by massive granite orthostats. There seems to be little local interest in it. Some said it is an old mine adit, but in the absence of a nearby mine and its immovable termination this seems unlikely! It seems to have attracted the usual 'secret tunnel' stories. A woman from the village told a tale that as a girl once she and some friends attempted to see if they could break through the great slab at the rear of the chamber. The tapping of their hammers was eerily met with a corresponding tap issuing from the other side. The excavation was quickly abandoned.

To me the Pisky's Hall has always held an aura of mystery, perched on a rise over Bosahan woods looking towards the north of the parish where the cyclopean Tolmen stone once stood. Although it is situated in an open field next to the road, it is notoriously difficult to find. It is also, as its name suggests, renowned for its otherworldly activity.

At the turn of the last century in his perambulation through the Celtic countries in search of faery lore, W Y Evans Wenz ("The faery faith in Celtic countries" – 1911) found the fogou whilst passing through the parish of Constantine and came across an informant who told him a tale of the Piskies hall. It is also interesting to note that the name of the area on which the fogou stands is known as Bosahan (said B'zain), which could translate from the Cornish as the holy/sacred house.

> *"At pisky house – William murphy, who married my sister (of Evans Wenz's informant, seventy eight year old John Wilmet), once went to the Pisky-house at Bosahan with a surveyor, and the two of them heard such unearthly noises in it that they came running home in great excitement, saying that they had heard the Piskies."*

Once in the 1990s I visited the fogou with a friend, who was herself of a particularly fey disposition. On entering the fogou, she instantly informed me that "They" had been active here. On enquiring as to who "They" might be she just replied "Them" and pointed to a perfectly formed bare human footprint all of three inches long in the mud.

Some years later I sat with a group of friends in the chamber of the fogou to await the setting of the winter solstice sun. At this time of year, it is rare for both the field and the sky to be clear, but this particular year the gods blessed us with an open view to the south west. After what seemed an age squatting on the dark earth with the great stones of the fogou wall at our backs, the sun set over the corner of the field sending a shaft of golden light piercing the entrance of the fogou and illuminating the chamber. For a moment the mysteries of the undying sun and the slumbering earth were united.

The fogous were the last in the line of the great prehistoric megalithic monuments to be built. As the sun set on the darkest day through the fogou door long ago, one cannot help but think that the ancient people who once built the fogou knew that it was the dawn of a new age in which we were becoming slaves to the fields of battle and the fields of agriculture. Maybe somewhere deep in our ancestral memory was a yearning for the caves of the Palaeolithic age where the gods and the spirits still spoke to us as we began our journey away from Eden. Maybe the fogou was a shrine to the memory of this cultural womb from whence we came.

Or maybe they embody an even deeper mystery. The ancient Celts believed that at the heart of the physical world was "Anwyn". Some described this as being the "Underworld", others of a more philosophical persuasion have described it as being the embodiment of absolute negation and otherness.

The Epicureans taught that the world of matter was constructed from the solid building blocks of "atoms" and Aristotle told us that nature abhors a vacuum...but post-Einstein both these mainstays of our western world view have fallen apart. Within what we thought were solid atoms, all we have found is a great yawning emptiness...it appears we got it the wrong way around! Nature abhors solid mass, in fact the very fact that solid mass exists at all has become something of a puzzle for modern physicists. Moreover, all that we thought to be solid matter is but a shimmer or a mirage on the face of the void, a dance of subatomic particles spontaneously coming and going, in and out of existence.

Much ink has been spilled in discourses on the construction and orientation of the fogou and of what once lay within, but maybe this is missing the point. When one crawls down from the upper-world and descends into the darkness of the fogou, one loses awareness of the stones of the chamber and the landscape beyond. One enters the liminality of Anwyn; a veil recedes, and the true nature of the fogou is made evident. The true fogou is not the stones that encase it but the space and the darkness within. The fogou is the darkness. As one surrenders to the living shadow of the chamber one is consumed by something more profound than just the absence of light, one glimpses the incomprehensible fifth dimension that lays beyond the fragile veil of 'being'...that space which is both nothing and everything.

To loose oneself in the fogou is to participate in this great paradox - that at the heart of 'being' is Anwyn, absence...the void.

Winter Solstice light enters the chamber of Pisky's Hall Fogou. Pic: Steve Patterson

The Stone Men of St Cleer

George Basil Barham

A thousand feet above sea level among the heather and bracken of Craddock Moor, four or five miles north of Liskeard, you may find to-day the remains of three ancient stone circles known as "The Hurlers." Antiquaries will tell you that the Druids first erected them, but the people of the countryside know better. From father to son, from grandparent to child, through long centuries, the story has been handed down of how "The Hurlers" came to be fixed in eternal stillness high up there above the little village of St. Cleer.

Exactly how long ago it was nobody knows, but it happened in those early days when pious saints were settling down in the remote parts of savage Cornwall and striving to convert the wild Cornish from their pagan ways.

Then, as even to this day, the game of Hurling - a sort of primitive Rugby football - was a popular pastime with the people. Village used to play against village, with goals perhaps four or five miles apart. And the good folk of St. Cleer were as fond of the game as any of their neighbours · so fond, in fact, that they would play it on any and every occasion, despite the admonitions of their local saint and parson, after whom the village was named.

Again and again, he would notice that his little church was empty on Sunday mornings while the shouts and noise of a hard-fought Hurling match drifted across the moorland in through the open church door. Again and again, he would take his flock to task for their godless ways and their Sabbath-breaking games. But it was of little use. For a Sunday or two they would be penitent and attend service. Then would come a fine morning, and a challenge perhaps from the Hurlers of St. Ive or North Hill, on the other side of the moors, and the young men would decide to chance another lecture from the patient saint, and out they would go to the hillside to do battle for the honour of their parish.

But even the patience of saints comes to an end at last, and good St. Cleer saw something more than words was needed to lead his people into the right way. And so, it happened one Sunday morning, in the midst of a hot tussle on Craddock Moor, the outraged St. Cleer arrived in search of his erring flock.

He bade them cease their game at once and return to church. Some of them obeyed, wandering sheepishly off down the hill; some were defiant and told the worthy man to go back to his prayers and not to come up there to spoil sport.

Then St. Cleer spoke in anger. Raising his staff, he told them in solemn and awful tones that it should be as they had chosen. Since 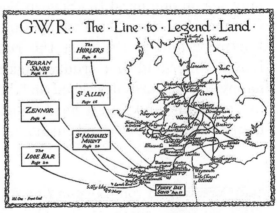 they preferred their game on the moor to their service in church, on the moor at their game they should stay for ever. He lowered his staff and to the horror of all onlookers the defiant ones were seen to be turned into stone.

Many centuries have passed since then. Time, wind and rain have weathered the stone men out of all semblance of humanity. Some have been destroyed, but

85

most still remain as an awful example to impious Sabbath profaners. And there you may see them silent and still, just as they were struck on that grim Sunday in the dark long ago.

The glorious moorland, rugged and wild, stretches all about them—a wonderful walking country, where one may escape from all cares and wander for hours amid the bracken and sweet-smelling grasses and find strange prehistoric remains seldom visited by any but the moorland sheep and the wild birds. It is a country of vast spaces and far views. You may see on one hand the Severn Sea, on the other the Channel; to the east the upstanding blue hills of Dartmoor and to the west the rugged highlands by Land's End—and then trudge back at night weary but happy to Liskeard, described as "the pleasantest town in Cornwall," and find it hard to believe that only five hours away is the toil and turmoil of London.

From *Legend Land: Being a collection of some of the Old Tales told in those Western Parts of Britain served by The Great Western Railway.* Published one hundred years ago, this was one of the first traveller companion *'visitor lore'* publications, written explicitly to enhance the holiday makers stay. Published in 1922 and written by George Basil Barham under the pen name of Lyonesse.

Donald R. Rawe and the 'Night on Roughtor'

Karen F. Pierce

I was first introduced to the Cornish writer Donald R. Rawe, and this story in particular, after attending a talk given by Alex Langstone where I queried whether there was any folklore connected with sleeping out on Roughtor. I've been conducting research on a variety of sites within Wales where legends state that to spend the night at a particular location will result in one awaking the next morning as a poet or insane, or if really unlucky one will not awaken at all. These locations tend to fall into two categories; mountains or burial chambers.[61] The legend connected to Cadair Idris (the Chair of Idris), a mountain within Snowdonia, is perhaps the most well known and was first recorded in c1600.

> "*And on the highest crown of this mountain is a bed-shaped form as it were, great in length and width, built of slabs or stones fixed around it. And this is called The Bed of Idris, though it is more likely that it is the grave in which Idris was buried in ages past. And it is said that whoever lies and sleeps on that bed, one of two things will happen to him, either he will be a poet of the best*

---

[61] It could be argued that prehistoric burial chambers are representations of mountains or hills and thus these two categories are essentially the same.

kind, or go entirely demented." Sion Dafydd Rhys (*The Giants of Wales and Their Dwellings*: Peniarth MS 118 f.829-837)

So far, I have only researched these legends in Wales but I am curious to know where else they appear in Britain. Listening to Langstone's talk about Cornish folklore it seemed that Roughtor and Brown Willy might be possible candidates for such a legend, and so I eagerly turned to Rawe's story. Although a piece of fiction rather than a straight retelling of folklore, he has woven many of the folkloric legends concerning Roughtor and the surrounding area into the narrative.

The tale involves three young men who spend the night of Midsummer Eve camping on the top of Roughtor,[62] despite the warnings of a local woman not to do so. As 'modern' men they are dismissive of folklore and superstition, but soon find out they were foolish not to pay attention to local legend. By the following morning they have suffered a variety of injuries, one of them is practically catatonic and another is lost on the moors for two days.

This story was first published in 1980 in *Haunted Cornwall* edited by Denys Val Baker, and later reprinted in Rawe's own 1994 collection *Haunted*

---

[62] Nothing is particularly emphasised about the date within the story, aside from Mrs Tregellas' initial warning about visiting Roughtor that night, although Rawe obviously picked it deliberately. Midsummer's Eve, or St John's Eve is traditionally celebrated with bonfires such as those lit on Carn Brea. To learn more about the significance of these fires see Hutton (1996: 311-321). In Wales it was known as one of the three 'spirit nights' (*y tair ysbrydnos*), and at Tinkinswood burial chamber one was warned not to sleep there on this night: "*...for the person who did so would die, go raving mad, or become a poet.*" Trevelyan (1909: 126)

Landscapes.[63] It is set in the late 1960s, thus in the recent past at the time of publication. Not that long ago, showing that the 'unexplained' is still happening, but having some distance for the reader who might think it wouldn't happen to them.[64]

Of the three men only one, McMahon, is shown to be of Cornish descent, and it could be argued that he fares the least worst out of all of them.[65] The distinction is clearly made in the story that the young men are 'English' and 'modern' whilst the housekeeper, Mrs Tregellas, who tells them about the local legends is 'Cornish' and stuck in the past.

"McMahon got up, smiling. 'You Cornish are all the same: living in the past, born with your heads looking over your shoulders. All these legends and mysteries are all very picturesque, but they won't get you anywhere. I consider it'll be a bit of a lark to pitch camp on Roughtor on Midsummer Night..." (p. 75)

Mrs Tregellas warns them repeatedly about spending the night on Roughtor, she calls it dangerous and sacrilegious, and highlights that none of the locals would set foot on it after sundown. The more she mentions local superstitions, the more they counteract her beliefs with their rationality and science, and the more they are encouraged to do just what she is warning them against. They see themselves as

---

[63] All page number references refer to the 1994 imprint.

[64] M. R. James (1924) notes that; *"For the ghost story a slight haze of distance is desirable. 'Thirty years ago,' 'Not long before the war', are very proper openings."*

[65] He calls himself English despite having a half Irish father and a French mother.

89

educated men who know better than the superstitious local woman. The characters are shown to represent opposites – in social class, education, age, and gender – and rather stereotypically drawn. With this genre you expect the crass protagonists to get their comeuppance and the beauty is in the telling.

The three men make their way to the top of Roughtor with their camping equipment, by the time they have pitched their tent they have already had some minor experiences which have caused them some disquiet. Left alone for a while McMahon has surveyed the surrounding landscape, and what would look mundane in daylight takes on a more mysterious hue in the twilight. Shadows creeping across the sides of hills are described as grey ghosts. A nearby stone circle looks poised to spring into life, for the stones to "shuffle and dance" and he half recalls a story about "*maidens changed into stones for dancing on the Sabbath*" (p. 78). This is probably a reference to Fernacre, a circle which lies below Roughtor, and is one of the largest in Cornwall.[66] Although it is not one of the many circles whose name originates from a petrification legend, there are several other circles in the vicinity, and over towards Hawk's Tor are the Trippet Stones which are believed to be named from the delicate footwork of a dancer.[67] He also finds the Logan Rock, a rocking stone. Standing on the tor, McMahon becomes aware of the landscape surrounding him. He is no longer in a safe and civilised environment but is surrounded by a land

[66] See Burl (1995:32) and Burnham (2018: 46).
[67] See Burl (1995: 37-38) and Burnham (2018: 48). For a theory about the three circles (Fernacre, Stannon, Louden) in the lee of Roughtor mirroring the tor itself see Goutté (2018).

that is "ageless, barbaric, primitive". He has stepped outside of his known world and trespassed where he shouldn't have and begins to feel the weight of millennia upon him.

The other two, Browne-Smythe and De Vere Ellis, witness a will o' the wisp, the 'Jacky Lantern' that Mrs Tregellas mentioned, and even though they know

Roughtor from Fernacre Stone Circle. Pic: Karen F. Pierce

it to be marsh gas they are slightly unsettled by the appearance of the dancing "purple ghost".

The atmosphere builds, and even though for the moment everything seen has an explanation or is real, nerves become frayed. The moon is full and described as "ominously amber"; the appearance in torch light of a white face with two large horns, is just a goat. Browne-Smythe realises how easy it would be for a man to go mad on those moors, where even in moonlight what is seen is only half seen:

"The moon cast enough light to present those gaunt shapes, grey enigmas, but never enough to explain them." (p. 81)

Finally, the three men drift off to sleep, only to be awoken by singing and laughing. It is from this point onwards in the story that what is seen cannot be explained by shadows or moonlight, and the fact that the men had fallen to sleep gives scope for their visions to perhaps be explained as nightmares. They investigate the sounds and find a circle of fifty small dancers, no taller than two feet high, wearing pointed caps of light green and blue. They are dancing around a boulder on which are sat three figures who are leading the singing, with the dancers joining in on the chorus. The young men don't understand the language being sung in, with McMahon initially thinking it was Welsh, before realising it had to be Cornish. As a prelude to the main events of the night, this scene was delightful and joyous, however it was not to last. Clouds cover the moon and in the darkness the singing and dancing cease, once the moon reappears there is a different set of little figures wearing caps of black and dark blue, ugly figures that are fighting and tripping one another up. These figures spot the young men and start towards them. McMahon flees, De Vere Ellis hesitates, and Browne-Smythe tries to run but trips up. Browne-Smythe is attacked but De Vere Ellis manages to rescue him. They all manage to escape back to the tent which by great fortune they have pitched by the remains of the chapel to Michael the Archangel, thus rendering them some protection.

The weather begins to play its part in adding to the atmosphere, the wind rises so much it sets the Logan Stone rocking, creating a soundtrack of a wild oscillating clunking. A storm rolls in and within the thunder and lightning they witness a giant figure repeatedly bending then throwing something over its shoulder, and they perceive this to be Jan Tregeagle bailing out Dozmary Pool – a story that Mrs Tregellas had mentioned to them earlier.[68] De Vere Ellis finds it difficult to comprehend all that he is seeing, and the strain begins to get to him. In an interchange between them McMahon shouts at him:

"You can't accept the supernatural; that's what's the matter with you. I've seen it: I believe and keep sane. You've seen it and you won't believe it: if you don't look out you'll go out of your mind!"
(p. 86)

As the storm intensifies, guy ropes snap and their tent collapses. They drag the remains of the tent and their belongings into the shallow protection of a cave under the Chapel rock. This leaves them in the perfect position to witness Jan Tregeagle being chased by hell hounds across the moor, between the two hills of Roughtor and Brown Willy. Just when they think the spectacle has moved far away Tregeagle and the pack chasing him return. De Vere Ellis runs away, Browne-Smythe attempts to do the same whilst McMahon tries

---

[68] See Langstone (2017: 165-167) for further details about Jan Tregeagle.

to get him to stay, emphasising that their current location is the only safe spot. However, Browne-Smythe lashes out in terror and McMahon is ultimately knocked unconscious. He awakens the next morning, his head covered in cuts and bruises and eventually locates Browne-Smythe who at this point is mute and has no memory. De Vere Ellis is missing for two days, once recovered he states a conviction that he was being led in circles all that time and was amazed not to have drowned in a bog. This is the last folkloric reference that Rawe makes in the story and is a nod towards the stories of people being pisky-led, such as that of Jan Brewer told by Enys Tregarthen.[69]

Rawe's story is constructed like many classic antiquarian ghost stories are, although the supernatural that the characters are dealing with here aren't necessarily ghosts. Moshenska (2021) notes that the protagonists in these tales are normally male scholars and that there is usually a character warning them against their actions who is always ignored:

> *"...often because their warnings are given in the language of folklore, which the antiquarian dismisses as mere superstition, and often because they are a simple peasant, a superstitious 'native', or a woman."* (Moshenska 2021: 17)

Mrs Tregallas fits this 'Cassandra archetype' very well, being the anthropological other to the young men, outside their cultural and social norms. They in

---

[69] Tregarthen (1906: 51-149-157).

turn conform to the scholar stereotype and are duly punished for their transgressions.

McMahon is also a figure torn between his Cornish roots and his educated English life, although in one respect he has already put his heritage firmly behind him, not even recognising Cornish when he hears the piskies singing in it but mistaking it for Welsh. He still manages to dredge up some memories of local folklore and is able to correctly identify the piskies and the spriggans. In the end though he does reject the Cornish part of himself, preferring not to return to Cornwall if he can help it, even though he ultimately owns the property there.

Although the story doesn't match up with the Welsh legends I've been investigating, with none of the participants ending up inspired as poets, they do very nearly go insane, with De Vere Ellis veering towards that way on the night, and Browne-Smythe's brain essentially shutting down and blocking out the pertinent memories. De Vere Ellis does however end up being inspired to study parapsychology and becomes an expert in the subject.

In some ways, as I mentioned above, the night on the tor feels split into two halves. Prior to sleep the men are dealing with real things that seem a bit spooky in the twilight; post falling asleep they are disturbed by happenings that are more nebulous. The concrete items in the first half of the night are locations which readers of Rawe's story could visit and help to ground the tale in reality. From the tor itself, full of archaeological riches of neolithic, bronze age and medieval remains, to the Logan Rock, and a stone circle (possibly Fernacre, although there are others in the area). Even St

95

Michael's chapel, which although they didn't realise was initially there, was the site they were drawn to camp at.

Once they have passed through the realm of sleep we are led into a world of piskies and spriggans, ghosts and hell hounds. These figures come from tales found in the collections of folklorists like Enys Tregarthen, Margaret Courtney, and Robert Hunt, and we can perhaps assume that Rawe was attempting to bring them to a wider audience. Rawe himself had published more traditional retellings of folk tales previously, such as his *Traditional Cornish stories and rhymes* in 1972.[70] This included the tale of Jan Tregeagle, and even more interestingly 'The Pisky who lost his laugh', who whilst searching for it on Bodmin Moor encounters Jack o'Lanterns, Tregeagle, and the Spriggans of Roughtor amongst others. The story also starts and ends with a large group of piskies dancing on the moors around a central fiddler. Rawe's pisky story is, in turn, a retelling of Enys Tregarthen's 'The adventures of a Piskey in search of his laugh' featured in her *North Cornwall fairies and legends* collection published in 1906. This story must have been one of the inspirational starting points for the 'Night on Roughtor' but with very different audiences in mind.

The pisky stories, and the 'Night on Roughtor' both encompass a couple of key factors. Firstly, they are stories which contain within them other stories, or allusions to other tales. They are frameworks upon

---

[70] In the preface he pays homage to folklorists who have gone before him: "*Robert Hunt (1865-77), M.A. Courtney (1890), J.H. Harris (1906), Enys Tregarthen (1906-10) and others. To those 'gatherers of fragments, that they be not lost', we owe an incalculable debt.*"

which to hang a series of possibly otherwise unconnected tales. 'Night on Roughtor' is about three men spending the night on the tor and the supernatural occurrences they witness – but within that we are led to a number of folktales. Both versions about the pisky looking for his laugh include him encountering several characters, such as Lady Want the mole, Jan Tregeagle, Merlin the tiny bargeman, and King Arthur the chough. These other tales have been brought into the pisky tale and connected by his journey but stand alone outside this story too.

Secondly, aside from the protagonist(s) and their journey, the other connecting factor is location. 'Night on Roughtor' is obviously focussed on Roughtor and its immediate vicinity, and Rawe has brought together all the folkloric elements and motifs that can be tied to this location. The pisky tales encompass a wider area, as the pisky is travelling looking for his laugh, but all are still located within a certain part of North Cornwall, and specific locations are mentioned throughout his travels. Tregarthen's version starts and ends at Tintagel Castle, with visits to Roughtor Marsh, Dozmary Pool, and Trebetherick Bay. Whilst in Rawe's telling we begin at Trevose Head, and the journey encompasses St Breock Downs, Bodmin Moor, Dozmary Pool, Roughtor and King Arthur's Halls. The particular characters that are met in both stories have ties to these specific locations.

As an introduction to the folklore surrounding Roughtor the story provides a good basis, weaving the tales into the landscape and intimating how some might have emerged from atmospheric conditions like marsh gas and storms. Even Mrs Tregellas grudgingly suggests that the hell hounds and the wild hunt might just be the weather.

Rawe is, however, also firmly rooting the folklore with place. He has used what was formerly included in children's tales to create atmosphere in this supernatural tale. It sits alongside ghost stories and occult tales but is also a useful exercise in bringing awareness to the folklore of North Cornwall. Finally, the message is one of respect – this is a sacred landscape, and one should take heed of local legends and not trespass where the piskies might get you on a 'spirit night'.

Bibliography

Burl, Aubrey (1995) *A guide to the stone circles of Britain, Ireland and Brittany.* New Haven: Yale University Press.

Burnham, Andy (2018, ed.) *The old stones: a field guide to the megalithic sites of Britain and Ireland.* London: Watkins.

Goutté, Roy (2018) 'The Rough Tor triangle: a theory.' In, Andy Burnham (ed.), *The old stones: a field guide to the megalithic sites of Britain and Ireland,* 44-45, London: Watkins.

Hutton, Ronald (1996) *The stations of the sun: a history of the ritual year in Britain.* Oxford: Oxford University Press.

Langstone, Alex (2017) *From Granite to Sea: The Folklore of Bodmin Moor and East Cornwall.* London: Troy Books.

James, M. R. (1924) 'Introduction', in V. H. Collins (ed.), *Ghosts and marvels: A Selection of Uncanny Tales from Daniel Defoe to Algernon Blackwood,* v-xvi, London: Oxford University Press.

Moshenska, Gabriel (2021) 'The realm of ancient terrors.' *Hellebore* 5 (Beltane): 13-19.

Rawe, Donald R. (1972) *Traditional Cornish stories and rhymes.* Truro: Lodenek Press.

Rawe, Donald R. (1994) *Haunted landscapes: Cornish and West Country tales of the supernatural.* Truro: Lodenek Press.

Tregarthen, Enys (1906) *North Cornwall fairies and legends.* London: Wells Gardner, Darton & Co.

Trevelyan, Marie (1909) *Folk-lore and folk-stories of Wales.* London: Elliot Stock.

Book Review: The Cornish Folklore Collection. Vol. 1

A brand-new compendium of folklore relating to Cornish and West Country witchcraft, charming and superstition is now available exclusively from Amazon. Edited by Kelvin I. Jones, and with contributions from many well-known researchers, including Graham King, Steve Patterson, and Alan M. Kent. Containing an expansive and thorough set of all manner of spells and charms, from across the 16th to 20th centuries, and brought together as an appealing and informative collection. Despite a broad content listing, the volume does not have any index, which is frustrating for researchers. However, this

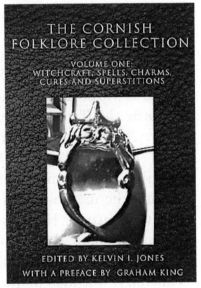

is a useful addition to the theme, and whilst I am pleased to see this in print, I really feel that the weighty size of the paperback will not withstand the test of time. I sincerely hope that the publisher will consider a decent hardback edition, which would grace the bookshelves of upcoming folklorists, far into the future. Never-the-less, I await the rest of the series with anticipation. *Alex Langstone*

The St Allen Piskies

Alex Langstone

The parish of St Allen lies within an area of green rolling hills north of Truro, with the River Allen rising at Ventoneage, close to St Allen Churchtown, flowing south towards Truro, where it joins the River Kenwyn to form the Truro River. The river name in Cornish *Dowr Alen* means shining river and shares its name with another Cornish River in the Camel Valley. Nothing is known about the patron saint, but it is thought he may have arrived from Brittany in the 6th or 7th century. He has been linked to 6th century Breton Bishop Alain of Quimper, who was originally from Wales. Traditionally his feast was held on 22 February, but also at Rogation (25 April). The church was built around 1190 and was recorded as Eglossalen in 1235.

There are three early medieval wayside crosses in the churchyard, two of which were discovered buried close to the church, the third (page 101) was brought from Trefronick Farm, during 1911, where it was discovered being used as a doorstep.

The hamlet and farmstead of Trefronick hosts some interesting and unusual piskie folklore, collected from a St Allen resident by Robert Hunt in 1835, and expanded upon by George Basil Barham, writing under the pen name of 'Lyonesse' in the *GWR Legend Land* series, which was published in 1922. It concerns the temporary loss of a child to the land of the piskies. The version below is my interpretation of the folktale.

One sunny afternoon, a small child was playing on the woodland edge, close to his family home by Trefronick Farm, St Allen. He was always interested in the natural world, and his father had taught him all about the wildflowers that grew in the vicinity, and the names of the songbirds that frequented the farm and woodland. The boy had found a particularly interesting patch of wild and herby flowers growing on the edge of the wood and was fully immersed in remembering their names. Soon after he heard a joyful tune emerging from the woodland, and at first wondered what bird could be producing such music. Though he quickly realised that this was no birdsong and began to wonder who was playing such sweet melodies from the woodland. He began to lose interest in the herbs and flowers he had been studying and began to move closer to the woodland edge. As he did so, the music became louder and more pronounced and he started to walk faster toward to source of the melodious sound.

Before long he found himself in a beautiful green grove, full of mature and majestic trees. The music had stopped, but he felt so comfortable and welcome in this spot, he continued his journey into the heart of the wood. As he went deeper into the forest, the thickly laid briars and bracken seemed to be laid flat before him as to make a pathway to an unknown destination. Soon the boy came to a shimmering, sparkling lake, and he sat down and stared into the waters. As he did so, the sky darkened and the sky became filled with starry constellations, of which he did not recognise. He quickly became weary and found a soft mound of moss and ferns where he quietly drifted off to sleep.

When he awoke, he found himself in a beautiful building, with glorious arches that soared up to the sky and which were encrusted with shining crystals of every colour. Standing beside him was a lady, who proceeded to guide the boy through the rooms of the ethereal palace, along with a procession of piskies who sang strange fascinating songs whilst they marched along behind the lady.

The piskies were very kind to the boy and treated him to a feast of the most wonderful tasting food, and when he became tired, they made him a bed from the softest moss and foliage they could muster.

Front cover of Great Western Railway's The Line to Legend Land No. 4.
Published 100 years ago and featuring the lost child of St Allen folktale.

Meanwhile the boy's parents had been searching for their son, and three days had passed where he just could not be found. Then on the morning of the third day, he just reappeared sleeping on a bed of ferns at the edge of the wood by the flowers he had been studying.

As Robert Hunt states in his recollection –

There was no reason given by the narrator why the boy was "spirited away" in the first instance, or why he was returned. Her impression was, that some sprites, pleased with the child's innocence and beauty, had entranced him. That when asleep he had been carried through the waters to the fairy abodes beneath them; and she felt assured that a child so treated would be kept under the especial guardianship of the sprites for ever afterwards. Of this, however, tradition leaves us in ignorance.

George Basil Barham's account of the tale ends with this:

And so it was; the boy lived to a ripe old age and prospered amazingly. He never knew illness or misfortune and died at last in his sleep; and those that were near him say that as he breathed his last a strange music filled the room.

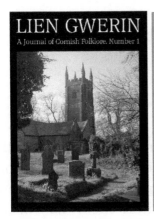

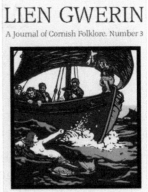

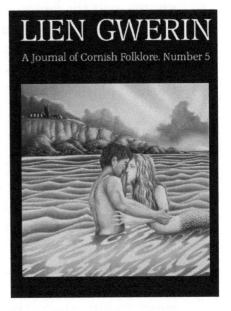

Lien Gwerin back issues are available from:

www.spiritofalbionbooks.co.uk

About the authors

Merv Davey

Merv Davey comes from a family rooted in Cornish folk tradition. His great grandmother used to play for dances on the fish cellars at Newquay in the 1880s and his grandfather was a step dancer. Merv has been involved in a variety of Cornish folk bands and dance groups over the years and helped to research the music and dance for these groups. A spell in a pipe band in the 1980s confirmed a passion for bagpipes which he has since transferred to the medieval variety including the Cornish pipes.

Alan M. Kent

Dr Alan M. Kent was born in St Austell and grew up in industrial mid-Cornwall. He is a Senior Lecturer in Literature with the Open University in South-West Britain and a Fellow in Celtic Studies at the University La Coruña, Galicia. He has published extensively on the literature, theatre and folklore of Cornwall. His most recent works include co-editing The Charter Fragment and Pascon agan Arluth (2020), The Mouth of Truth (2021) and Saffron-Bun Chapel (2021).

Alex Langstone

Publisher, author, esoteric explorer, and editor of this journal. Writing primarily about place, his work focusses upon folklore, magic, the paranormal, occult topography, and the Genius-Loci. His 2017 book, *From Granite to Sea*, is a comprehensive exploration of the folklore of Bodmin Moor and eastern Cornwall. He is currently writing a companion book to the above-mentioned volume, which will focus on the folkloric, mythic, and enchanted landscapes of mid-Cornwall. www.alexlangstone.com

Steve Patterson

Steve Patterson is an author, woodcarver and folklorist who lives and works in an off-grid shack in an old granite quarry in west Cornwall. He is an auto-didactic outsider researcher, meta-antiquarian and artificer of strange and wonderful things. He has worked with the museum of witchcraft and magic in Cornwall since the mid 1990's. He currently runs the "Antiquarian adventures in Meta reality" podcast and is director of the *"Gwithti an Pystri – a cabinet of folklore and magic"* museum in Falmouth, Cornwall, which will be opening Easter 2022. www.stevepattersonantiquarian.com

Karen F. Pierce

Dr Karen F. Pierce is a cataloguing librarian and independent researcher based in South Wales. Her PhD was on Helen of Troy, and she is interested in folklore, mythology, and mythical interactions with the landscape. From 1998-2006 she was the editor of 'Drops of the Awen', the Pagan Federation regional magazine for South and Mid Wales. Curious about stone circles she embarked on a mission to visit 50 of them in Britain, writing up her experiences as she went along, this journey continues and the next 50 beckon. Her current research project explores the folklore of prehistoric sites.

Rupert White

Rupert White trained as a doctor at University College, London, before returning to live in his boyhood home of Cornwall, where he set up the online magazine artcornwall.org. Since 2010 he has written a series of books that explore separate, but overlapping, aspects of pre- and post-war cultural history. He is also the editor of *The Enquiring Eye: Journal of the Museum of Witchcraft & Magic.*

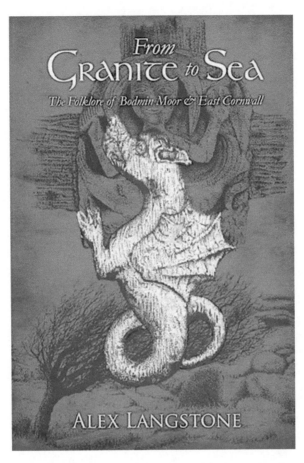

From Granite to Sea is the first book to comprehensively focus on the folklore of Bodmin Moor and eastern Cornwall. Available now from www.troybooks.co.uk

"Through this book the secrets of a landscape are revealed"
Elizabeth Dale (The Cornish Bird)

"Set to become a modern classic of the genre"
Museum of Witchcraft & Magic

"Evocative and atmospheric" *Meyn Mamvro*

L - #0072 - 170222 - C0 - 210/148/6 - PB - DID3270640